THE CLOUDED LENS

HOOVER INTERNATIONAL STUDIES
Richard F. Staar, director

THE PANAMA CANAL CONTROVERSY
Paul B. Ryan

THE IMPERIALIST REVOLUTIONARIES
Hugh Seton-Watson

SOUTH AFRICA: WAR, REVOLUTION, OR PEACE?
L. H. Gann and Peter Duignan

TWO CHINESE STATES
Ramon Myers, editor

THE CLOUDED LENS
James Noyes

THE CLOUDED LENS
Persian Gulf Security and U.S. Policy

JAMES H. NOYES

Foreword by William J. Porter

HOOVER INSTITUTION PRESS
Stanford University, Stanford, California

The Hoover Institution on War, Revolution and Peace, founded at
Stanford University in 1919 by the late President Herbert Hoover,
is an interdisciplinary research center for advanced study on
domestic and international affairs in the twentieth century. The views
expressed in its publications are entirely those of the authors
and do not necessarily reflect the views of the staff, officers,
or Board of Overseers of the Hoover Institution.

Hoover Institution Publication 206

*with love and appreciation
to my mother and father*

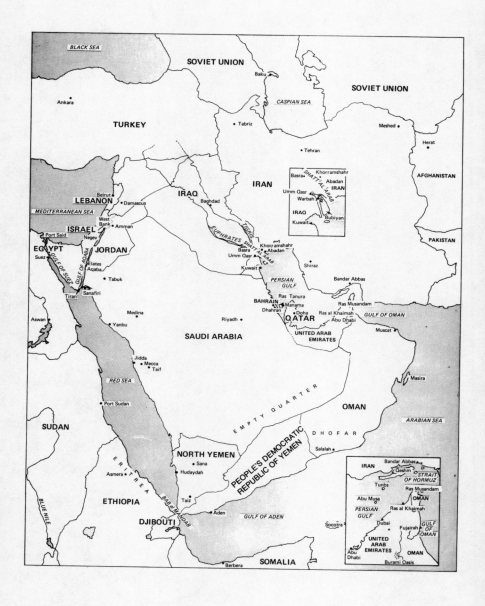

Contents

EDITOR'S FOREWORD   ix

FOREWORD   xi

ACKNOWLEDGMENTS   xiii

INTRODUCTION   xv

1. WHAT TO ASK FROM HISTORY   1
   From Antiquity to European Seapower   1
   Arab-Persian Relations   3
   The West's Forcible Entry   4
   Rule from the Sea Expands to Arms Control   6

2. BRITISH MILITARY RULE FLOURISHES AND PASSES   8
   Weapons Monopolies Fade   9
   Twilight Portents: Kuwait and Aden   10
   Changing Ideologies and Power   13
   The View from the West   14

3. REALITY VERSUS PREDICTION   17
   The Momentum of Healing: Buraimi Oases   18
   Back from the Brink: Iran and Iraq   19
   Cooperation Tested: The Dhofar Rebellion   20

4. WHY THE CLOUDED LENS   23
   The Mist of Thin Analogies   23
   British Rule Misread   25
   The Paradox of Post-Withdrawal Security   26

5. EVOLVING SECURITY CONCEPTS   29
   Toward Quiet Alliances   29

Military Prerequisites for Stability: Iran 31
Response to Military Challenges: Saudi Arabia 35
The Smaller Gulf States 39
Jordan: A Special Gulf Role 42

6. U.S. INTERESTS IN THE GULF 44
Oil and Security: Wartime Transition 44
A Habit Forms: Public Confusion on Energy 46
Energy Trends: Impact of the Soviet Equation 47
Gulf Power: Soviet Pressures 50

7. U.S. POLICY IN THE GULF: SUPPORTING U.S. INTERESTS 53
U.S. Imperial Presence or a Strengthened Gulf 54
Military Instruments of Foreign Policy 56

8. DEBATES ON U.S. GULF POLICY 60
Arms Sales Lead Policy 64
U.S. Policy Promotes Competition, Not Cooperation 67
The Policy is Unworkable in the Volatile and
Unstable Gulf 70
Gulf Arms Sales Threaten the Delicate Military
Balance in the Middle East 74
Arms Should Not Be Sold to Countries Unable
to Absorb Them 82
American Military Advisors Become Hostages
and Risk U.S. Military Involvement 86
The U.S. Should Prepare to Seize Gulf Oil, Not
Develop the Strength of Gulf Forces 90
Sophisticated Weapons in the Gulf Increase the
Risk of War and Are Militarily pointless 97
U.S. Military Support Contributes to
Political Suppression 102
The World Energy Crisis is Fictional 106

CONCLUSION 111
APPENDIX 115
NOTES 121
BIBLIOGRAPHY 133
INDEX 141

Editor's Foreword

This monograph, the fifth in our international studies' series, analyzes the dramatic transition made by the Persian Gulf countries from objects of strong colonial influence to complete independence. With the latter has come a mounting degree of cooperation among the states in the region. To many Western observers who had anticipated a tumultuous postcolonial era of rivalry and conflict this peaceful development has come as a surprise. The sudden emergence of the Gulf as a strategic world power center since 1973 has accelerated the process of historical evolution.

The author describes how this acceleration contributes to public confusion or misunderstanding about the Gulf and its significance for the economic and military strength of the noncommunist industrial world. Essentially a discussion of U.S. foreign policy, the book focuses in large part on military assistance and sales as policy instruments. Coupled with controversy over the analysis of U.S. weapons programs abroad, the author found himself compelled to include the equally contentious issues of global energy requirements. Furthermore, aspects of the Arab-Israeli confrontation are integral to any discussion of United States policy in the Gulf. The result is a book not only to inform and offer a set of conclusions but also to provoke thought and discussion.

A major contribution of this volume lies in its empathy for indigenous ideas about defense and security within the Persian Gulf states themselves. Historical perspective provides a view of how local leaders perceive security threats and how their approach to defense modernization has been strongly colored by earlier experience with friendly Western powers. This helps fill an information gap that became evident during the recent controversy over United States' arms sales to Saudi Arabia and Iran.

Important concern is reflected in this monograph for several broad issues of American foreign policy today. First of all, Soviet behavior in areas adjacent to the Gulf raises familiar doubts about its commitment to détente. Recent activities by the Soviet Union also point continuously to the question of future Bloc energy requirements and the potential military/political impact on Gulf stability. Second, the United States has not yet formulated to date any widely acceptable policy explanation for military assistance to areas like the Gulf that do not belong to NATO but whose security is linked integrally to that of the West. Complicating the task of gaining acceptance for such policy, of course, is the prominent attention given to strategic as well as conventional arms limitation efforts. Finally, there exist the intricacies of forging a mature political relationship with the Gulf countries, which help in their defense modernization implies. At the same time, the United States must cope with adversary positions on the OPEC front. The Gulf perhaps is the most important test area for partnership between the West and the Third World countries that control strategic resources.

RICHARD F. STAAR
Director of International Studies Program
Stanford, California   *Hoover Institution*

Foreword

James H. Noyes is well fitted by experience and perception to write this book on Persian Gulf security and U.S. policy. For much of the time over the past decade he occupied a position at the policymaking level of the U.S. government, and he gained particular recognition for his work on U.S. politico-military relations with the countries bordering the Gulf.

Having decided to produce a comprehensive study of this subject, James Noyes has done more than that: This is a definitive work, for which historians, statesmen, working-level scholars, and business organizations will be grateful. The great scope of his work will be particularly appreciated by those who have labored both in the Gulf area and in Washington, D.C., to develop and execute a cautious and sane policy aimed essentially at enhancing the security of the moderate Gulf States while reinforcing, if required, the probability of access by the West to their oil resources. The entire canvas, as it now stands, tends to vindicate those who formed, advocated, and applied our policy for the Gulf region, despite the resistance of those who considered it to be unworkable and the world energy crisis, fictional.

In approaching his main topics, the author provides us with a very useful combination of history and his own practical view of events in the 1960s and seventies. In justifying U.S. military-associated measures in the region, James Noyes painstakingly works on point after point, providing rebuttals extensively when dealing with those who opposed the policies with which he was associated, or of which he approved. In that connection, his chapters on "U.S. Policy in the Gulf: Supporting U.S. Interest" and "Debates on U.S. Gulf Policy" deserve special attention. His discussions of the particular problems of Saudi Arabia and the other xiiTHE CLOUDED LENS

Gulf states and U.S. policy toward their needs should, I believe, gain the approbation of reasonable men.

Most readers will form their own opinions as they proceed through this formidable book, but they will also find James Noyes's own conclusions worth pondering. He believes harder tests of the soundness of U.S. policy are still to be faced as social and political pressures come with change and evolution. He reaches the forthright position that "U.S. defense-related presence conveys at least a capability, if not always an offer of logistics support to the Gulf States in time of crisis," and he adds that though we would encounter "nightmarish" problems of inaccessibility (during an emergency), "U.S. capabilities would be equal to such a challenge," assuming there is a national will to meet it.

There are now approximately 75,000 Americans in the Persian Gulf area. These are involved in the modernization and military efforts of at least half a dozen countries, including three of primary importance to the United States—Saudi Arabia, Iran, and Kuwait. The timely arrival on the scene of this book will undoubtedly attract their attention and stimulate their thinking. It will be also a most useful reference work.

Most Americans moving toward the Gulf, either as organizations or individuals, need to know how our presence there developed and to have a good look at the interplay of factors involved in our present policy. James Noyes gives them all that in good and persuasive measure.

WILLIAM J. PORTER
*Former Undersecretary of State
for Political Affairs
and former Ambassador to Saudi
Arabia and Algeria*

Acknowledgments

Foremost appreciation is due the Earhart Foundation for the generous fellowship research grant enabling the full time commitment required for this study. Similarly indispensable was my appointment as Visiting Senior Fellow at the Institute of International Studies, University of California, Berkeley, where working space as well as a congenial atmosphere were graciously provided. I am particularly grateful to Professor Carl Rosberg, Director, and to Professor Robert Price, Associate Director.

My special thanks are owed to Thomas R. Mattair, Berkeley doctoral candidate in political science, for his rigorous and insightful work on the manuscript's first draft. Georgiana G. Stevens and Professor Joseph J. Malone generously devoted formidable talents and background to reading a subsequent draft as did Professor George Lenczowski, whose acuity and warm encouragement sustained the project from its inception. Their contributions are reflected in improved clarity throughout.

I am also deeply indebted to many friends in the Gulf countries who freely discussed the issues within this study and frequently offered warmhearted hospitality. To spare them perhaps unwanted association with delicate matters I have omitted their names. The same applies to former colleagues in government.

Finally, I should note my own acute awareness of the controversy surrounding the conventional designation of the Gulf as "Persian." As an American citizen I have gratefully left this question under the purview of the responsible national authority, the United States Board on Geographic Names.

Introduction

One of the more perverse manifestations of human behavior is the rejection and denigration of unwelcome new information. Rejection and denigration are most intense, usually, when the information has major policy implications—as was the case with developments in the Persian Gulf area after 1973. In the early stages of recovery from the divisive effects of the war in Vietnam, and in the midst of the obsessive Watergate process, the American public was called upon to face another painful foreign policy reality. For the first time in history, and with distressing rapidity, the United States was becoming dependent on foreign oil.

Worse still, the key reserves and potential increased production lay in the volatile and unstable Gulf area. It became clear that NATO would be unable to fight a conventional war of significant duration without assured access to Gulf oil. Consequently, vital American security interests had suddenly become extended to include a medieval area on the other side of the earth—a logistical nightmare in terms of defense, or, as urged in certain quarters, occupation by U.S. forces. Hence, even as a degree of consensus favored a reduction of security perimeters, a new and complex realization was, on the whole, rejected. The perversity of the reaction lay in part with its timing. Rejection followed the use of political and economic warfare by Gulf states against the Americans and their allies. To make matters worse, the spate of sensational writings on the subject has generally resulted in decreased public understanding.

Public concern over a Gulf power vacuum arose at the time of British military withdrawal in 1971 and was followed shortly by fear of a Gulf arms race, both exacerbated by the onset, after 1973, of the "petrodollar" era. More recently, other factors have complicated the task of relating the Gulf area to U.S. national interests. Presidential election politics in 1975–76 emphasized the arms sales issue. Amid the political rhetoric, distortions were inevitable. Moreover, it became clear that the fundamental problem of energy dependency in the U.S., which shapes U.S. attitudes toward the Gulf, is so beset with apparent contradictions as to defy confident analysis.

Further, assessments of Gulf developments are inexorably drawn into the labyrinthine Arab-Israeli dispute. Thus, distortions of another order are inevitable. A combination of factors more likely to promote public confusion on a subject could hardly be marshalled.

Only 50 years ago a British authority on the Gulf wrote: "Whatever of civilization and of public order exists to-day in these waters has its origin in the patient labors and generally unrewarded gallantry of successive generations of soldiers, seamen, and supercargoes, British and Indian. . . ."[1] Inevitably, 150 years of British hegemony not only inspire feelings of self-righteousness but conceal many deeper and more pervasive disputes and motivations of the region's peoples. Hence, not only an imperial but several indigenous historical and cultural legacies shape the attitudes of today's Gulf leaders as they look to security requirements. Certainly, independent nationhood and modernization are conceptually inseparable from an ability to meet Gulf defense needs without the ministrations of an imperial policeman. Our own judgments have tended to ignore the history of the area, as evidenced by the bulk of testimony during Congressional hearings beginning in 1972. Arms sales and other defense-related activity have been viewed primarily from the standpoint of the risks of U.S. involvement in new foreign conflicts. Almost unfailingly absent was a consideration of the risks for U.S. security through a policy of non-involvement in Gulf defense affairs.

Because of this self-centered approach, the Gulf's own natural defense interests often have been ignored. The evolving process of meeting security requirements in the area has been made to appear bizarre and somehow threatening to American interests. This coloration remains, in part, because time has obscured the significant U.S. role in Gulf security affairs initiated long before the departure of British military forces—through military assistance and support for Iran against post-World War II Soviet pressures. Most of all, however, current judgments frequently distort the subordinate nature of U.S. defense-related activities. The leading edge of American policy and presence in the Gulf remains economic and technological. Military assistance and sales in the area are not creatures of the oil embargo or possessed of a life of their own, independent of broader foreign policy. This study searches for perspective on the Gulf's origins, its current vital relationship to U.S. national security, and the purpose of U.S. security-related activities there. Many view the Gulf with panic. Others tend to ignore its full significance for Western interests. The need is to diminish both proclivities.

CHAPTER ONE

What To Ask From History

From Antiquity to European Seapower

The importance of the Persian Gulf area predates its current energy-related stature. As Sir Arnold Wilson wrote, 50 years ago, "No arm of the sea has been, or is of greater interest, alike to the geologist and archeologist, the historian and geographer, the merchant, the states-man, and the student of strategy, than the inland water known as the Persian Gulf."[2] This study is limited to only a few facets of the Gulf's long and complex history. First, to better understand the modern Gulf, we need to identify the major cultural forces existing in the area before the arrival of Europeans. This perspective is necessary to correct the distorted view that "whatever of civilization and public order exists in these waters today has its origins" in British or European efforts.

Second, for the understanding of Iranian-Arab rivalry, often cited as one of the major destabilizing forces in the region, it is important to review the ebb and flow of Persian and Arab power across the Gulf. How did history finally configure the pattern at the point of British departure in 1971? Was it, as in so many other areas, virtually to guarantee con-flict upon the departure of the colonial power? Or was the Gulf left in the more unusual condition of a generally acceptable equipoise between the logic of geography and the emotion of nationalisms? The answers to these questions are, of course, critical to an assessment of Gulf stability as well as to an assessment of the wisdom of assisting the key countries of the area to develop credible defense forces.

Third, we need to examine the means of entry employed by foreign powers in the Gulf between the early arrival of the Portuguese and the final departure of British forces. Superior weapons and distinctly

advanced military organization were essential elements in the foreigners' ability to control much of the region. This was particularly true
of naval forces. This background is important to understanding the
actions of the Gulf countries since 1971, as they moved quietly from the
era of British tutelage.

From earliest times, as today, the Gulf required local stability and
protected trade routes abroad in order to prosper. Established settlements were based on trade. More than 5,000 years ago, Bahrain thrived
as an entrepôt between the Indus Valley and the Sumerian city of Ur in
what is now southern Iraq. As Philip Hitti observes, "Like a thick wedge
the Arabian peninsula thrusts itself between the two earliest seats of
culture: Egypt and Babylonia . . . [and] the Panjab in India may have
been a third cultural focus."[3] Arabia Felix, or southern Arabia, so much
discussed by classical scholars, exploited its resources of frankincense,
spices, and myrrh, important for medicinal and religious purposes to the
Egyptians and Babylonians. The several successive great kingdoms that
resulted, flourished from seven centuries before the Christian era until
the Islamic period. Aside from development of sophisticated agricul-
ture, their prosperity depended on control of trade routes throughout
the Arabian peninsula, particularly the so-called Incense Trail. Successful exploitation of indigenous resources and a strategic location
depended in large part on the simple ability to protect caravans tra-
versing the area. Shipping had to be monopolized on the Red Sea route
that formed an alternate when the overland track through the Fertile
Crescent became increasingly threatened. Decline of the southern
Arabian kingdoms began when the Romans brought their own shipping
into the Red Sea. Roman motivation, according to Pliny, was based on
"the high prices exacted by the South Arabian traders for commodities
for which Rome had to pay in cash because she had so little to offer by
way of goods they desired."[4] This wry historical footnote is of possible
current relevance for Gulf oil ministers.

With the coming of Islam, the Persian Gulf and Gulf of Oman
eclipsed southern Arabia, becoming centers of a rapidly expanding commerce that probably achieved its zenith during the ninth century A.D.
Egyptian and Indian navigation and shipbuilding enabled Arab vessels
to withstand the monsoon winds. As a result, under the Umayyad and
Abbasid caliphs (A.D. 600–870) the sea route from the Persian Gulf to
Canton became "the longest in regular use by mankind before European
expansion in the sixteenth century, . . . a remarkable achievement."[5]

The unifying strength produced by these caliphs was matched in China by the Tang dynasty (A.D. 618–907) as trade flourished. Arabs remained the leading sailors and traders throughout the Indian Ocean to the end of the fifteenth century and the coming of the Portuguese.[6]

The great city-states that arose along the waters of the Persian side of the Gulf from the twelfth century on, Siraf, Qais, and Hormuz, were founded and controlled by Arabs, though much of the population was Persian. These city-states, including New Hormuz, which replaced Hormuz following its destruction during the Mongol invasion, "successively gained control of the Far-Eastern and African trade and became very rich in the process."[7] Essentially, "from the rise of Islam until the sixteenth century Moslems controlled the Middle East and monopolized trade with the East by land and sea."[8] The arrival of Vasco da Gama in the Indian Ocean in 1498 signaled the end of this Arab and Persian enterprise, just as the entry of Roman ships into the Red Sea brought the ultimate collapse of the earlier commercial role of southern Arabia. But the record is clear that Persian and Arab cultures of the Gulf area engaged in vigorous trade and enterprise for centuries prior to the coming of Europeans.

For the next several hundred years, there was a "struggle for trade and power in the Gulf in which Portuguese, English, Dutch, French and Turks all participated as well as Arabs and Persians," an "era of sea battles, fighting between the European powers and landings and attacks from the sea as well as exploitation of the rich trade of the East."[9] Such piracy, which ultimately provided British justification for control, was in part a consequence of the devastating inroads of European trade, then, and not the historic norm. As one authority notes, ". . . competition among the city states was ruthless and intense . . ." to the extent that "too often Western observers have confused these upheavals with simple, criminal piracy."[10]

Arab-Persian Relations

Historical perspective on the current issue of Arab-Iranian relations brings one analyst to the optimistic conclusion that "a remarkably balanced process of advance and withdrawal to and from both sides [of the Gulf] has taken place over the years, and that now the practical and historically supportable limits of irredentism have been reached."[11]

Hawley notes the "tradition of constant coming and going that there has always been throughout history between Oman and the Persian shore. Arab rulers have frequently controlled parts of Southern Persia, ruling independently at times of weak Persian government."[12] From the arrival of the Portuguese in 1507 until the departure of British forces in 1971, contested areas like Bahrain, Oman, and some Persian territory remained frozen within the imposed system of British order. Fortunately, the one surviving claim that could most quickly have inflamed all suppressed territorial issues in the Gulf—Iran's claim to Bahrain—was renounced in May 1970 following a U.N.-supervised review that resulted in Bahraini independence.

While contested issues remain, as will be described shortly, the Gulf entered the modern epoch in 1971 with its major Arab and Iranian populations configured in relative harmony with an historical logic that only chauvinists on both sides of the Gulf would dispute. In contrast to so many parts of post-colonial Africa and Asia, the residue of claims and counterclaims did not burden Gulf leaders with the virtual necessity of embedding the issues as central policy. The substantial numbers of Arabs who live in Iran are at least symbolically balanced by the large Iranian population inhabiting the states on the Arab side of the Gulf. In a real sense, ". . . now both parties are in possession of their 'natural' frontiers."[13]

The West's Forcible Entry

Finally, before considering current Gulf defense and security, it is useful to review the means of entry into the Gulf employed by Western powers. Wilson reminds us that "prior to the arrival of the Portuguese, the Arabs [of Oman and the Yemen] held control of the Eastern sea-borne trade which had for several centuries so enriched all who had a share in it. It was this control which the Portuguese wrested from them and succeeded in holding. . . ."[14] The process was ungentle. In 1506 Albuquerque seized the island of Socotra in order to block the Red Sea trading route. He then proceeded to the Gulf and systematically plundered ports and vessels, usually completing his visits by burning the remnants. Prisoners often had their noses and ears cut off.[15] But, "no power was ever master of the entire Gulf for any appreciable length of time," as Hay notes, citing Portuguese political and commercial dominance for around 100 years, after which they were expelled from Hormuz by the Persians with English help in 1622.[16] Their fate at Muscat at the hands of the Arabs was the same twenty-eight years later. From then until the middle of the eighteenth century, commercial rivalry between the Dutch and the British dominated the Gulf, until the Dutch finally left the field to the British. The Portuguese purpose had been to monopolize trade, and though they occupied forts in the Gulf and at times actually operated customs houses in Hormuz and Muscat, they were not colonizers.[17]

Nor were the British, whose interest in the Gulf increased as Napoleon conquered Egypt and then sent his army into Syria. A French fleet was launched on the Red Sea and the two principal routes to India were threatened. Trade, as always, was the key motivator, and by this time the flow of goods between Bombay and Muscat had become important, with the ships often manned by European officers.[18] This trade was not secure. European privateers had become active along with Indian and Arab pirates. The struggle for trade between the Qawasim (family name of the rulers of Sharjah and Ras al Khaimah) and the Omanis was disruptive. This battle was "partly based on tribal and factional differences, but above all the struggle was economic."[19] The Gulf had few resources and trade was a primary basis of income for the Qawasim, although defense of this trade was commonly called piracy. As one authority concedes, "Piracy, like treason, is a relative term."[20] The capture of two East India Company merchant brigs by the Qawasim in 1805 was followed in 1808 by an attack on the Company cruiser *Sylph* in which the Indian crew was slaughtered. The Qawasim then demanded that Bombay henceforth pay tribute to assure the safe passage of British ships.[21]

The Governor of Bombay responded in November 1809 by launching an East India Company expedition to Ras al Khaimah that killed some 300 Arabs and destroyed over 50 vessels and all the merchandise in the town. In style and purpose the mission resembled Albuquerque. The Company expedition then occupied Lingeh on the Persian side of the Gulf where some twenty vessels were also burned. This first British expedition resulted in suppression of Qawasim activity only until 1812 when new attacks began on the Company's shipping.

Qawasim vigor increased, and by 1819 the inevitable second British expedition of a much larger force included European and Indian troops as well as some 600 Arabs from neighboring Oman, whose ruler shared the British desire to suppress the Qawasim. Employing a method of war new to the area, the expedition utilized artillery barrages from ships and the beaches to destroy forts at Ras al Khaimah, Jazira al Hamra, Ajman, Umni al Qaiwain, Sharjah, and other smaller villages. More than 200 large vessels were captured or destroyed. Bahrain ports were blockaded.[22]

After several months the British point had been made and the way prepared for a "General Treaty of Pacification with the Arab sheikhs . . ." that "became the foundation of future policy in the Gulf and the origin of the special relationship . . . between Britain and the sheikhdoms of Trucial Oman."[23] A garrison remained at Ras al Khaimah under the command of a British captain who also served as political agent in the Gulf. The die was cast, and order was imposed thereafter, by force when necessary, until 1971. Superior weapons enabled the vastly outnumbered British, combined with Indian and other foreign manpower, to control the waters of the Gulf and, for the most part, the Indian Ocean. The lesson remains deep in the Gulf historical memory.

Rule from the Sea Expands to Arms Control

The guiding British principle of suppressing "piracy only" meant that British-led forces for the most part stayed off the mainlands of the Gulf. One notable breaching of this principle, in 1820, resulted in disaster for the British, whose effort did best at sea. After fifteen years of trying to maintain a military base on land in the Gulf, they abandoned Qishm as they had Ras al Khaimah, principally due to health problems and a desire to avoid the political quagmires on both sides of the Gulf. Although naval control only assured one aspect of peace, the British relied thereafter largely on their "watch and cruise" system.

British agreements and treaties from 1906 to 1923 were generally either maritime (1806–1853, maintaining peace and eliminating piracy and slave trade), political (1861–1916, involving broadened relationships between the Gulf sheikhdoms and the government of India), or economic (1902–1923, giving the British preferential rights and privileges for oil concessions, pearling, and postal/telegraph services).

Impetus for the safety and control of trade had effectively secured a strategic area for British purposes. These purposes evolved in the nineteenth century to include "upholding the independence of and territorial integrity of Persia and Afghanistan as buffer states between India and the expanding Russian dominions in Asia."[24] A British authority cited "the wholesale dissemination of fire-arms among the various peoples of the Gulf littoral," as a problem virtually equal to piracy and slave traffic.[25]

Arms from the Gulf became a factor in the Afghan Wars, and elaborate control measures culminated in 1912 with direct British handling of all arms shipments through an arms warehouse at Muscat. Significantly, therefore, possession of modern firearms was treated as largely a European privilege well into the twentieth century. Current Gulf attitudes toward the availability of modern weapons reflect this history.

CHAPTER TWO

British Military Rule Flourishes and Passes

British control of foreign affairs and defense matters tightened in the Gulf throughout the nineteenth century. The methods of imposing British will were simple—threat of bombardment, bombardment, or temporary occupation—and invariably successful because the objective was generally limited to reversal or denial of a specific action. In 1838 a British force from India occupied Kharg Island in response to a Persian siege against Herat, Afghanistan, apparently with Russian encouragement. Once the Shah withdrew in 1842, the British withdrew from Kharg Island. The sequence was repeated in 1856–57 with the additional British action of capturing other coastal points and conducting a naval bombardment of Mohammerah (now Khorramshahr). Persia then signed a treaty in Paris in 1857 agreeing not to meddle in Afghan affairs. When Bahrain was threatened by invasion from Qatar in 1859, encouraged by the Ottoman Turkish occupiers of the adjoining Hasa area, British warships attacked and destroyed or captured the boats assembled for the invasion off Qatar. Four years later, the Sultan of Muscat granted rights to the French for a coaling station there, in violation of his 1891 treaty with the British. This French push for influence was thwarted after British warships sat off Muscat for seven days until the Sultan cancelled his concession to the French. In 1920 British gunboats and military aircraft intervened to protect Kuwait from an attack by the Wahhabis of Saudi Arabia. In 1927 British aircraft bombed Saudi camps along Iraq's border in retribution for punitive Saudi raids.

Weapons Monopolies Fade

An evolution in the amounts and kinds of weapons available in the Arab world and Iran profoundly influenced British capabilities and became a factor arguing for British military withdrawal from its Gulf role. One authority attributes the much earlier end of Ottoman rule in the Arabian peninsula to Arab acquisition of firearms, and notes the transient superiority provided to the British by a monopoly on the rifle and the mountain gun in the nineteenth century.[1] These weapons were relatively easy to acquire, learn to use, and maintain. The aircraft, however, as Gavin notes, "was a rather different proposition. It could penetrate the most inaccessible fastnesses and was especially effective in semi-desert areas where it could easily pinpoint its target."[2] The air power monopoly in the Gulf served the British variously. In 1930 they even permitted Abd al Aziz al Saud, the founder of modern Saudi Arabia, to purchase four military aircraft. These were flown by hired British pilots to subdue rebellious Saudi Ikhwan tribal forces who had raided Iraqi forts on the Iraq-Nejd frontier.[3] British air power could accomplish, for a time then, the same kind of fleeting devastation as had been effected by European sea power centuries ago with such literally overwhelming results. World War II, combined with the psychological and military impact of the Arab defeat in the 1948 Palestine war, however, brought British exclusivity in air power to an end in the Gulf.

Independence for India in 1947, moreover, ended not only much of the rationale traditionally sustaining British purpose in the Gulf, but also meant that British forces now functioned alone at the end of a very long supply line. Fewer men faced ever-enlarging tasks. By 1955 British forces had to intervene in Oman's full-scale civil war to restore the Omani sultan's control. During the same year British forces also entered the complex Buraimi oases dispute between Saudi Arabia and Abu Dhabi, ultimately by helping force the Saudis from the oases. These interventions were only a beginning. Paradoxically, the British stake in Gulf oil mounted coincidentally with the growth of nationalist feelings in the Gulf on which Soviet proxy capabilities could play. The old treaty relationships had become encumbrances to the requirements of modern British diplomacy among the dominant Gulf states.

Twilight Portents: Kuwait and Aden

Two other episodes in the twilight of Britain's Gulf rule revealed how the imperial role had become in some instances unworkable and in others politically and financially overextended—the massive British response to Iraq's threat to absorb Kuwait in 1961 and the forced collapse of Britain's Aden Colony rule in 1967.

On June 19, 1961 the Ruler of Kuwait exchanged letters with the British government that established Kuwait as a fully independent state, bound to Britain only by a Treaty of Independence that included British preparedness to assist Kuwait if asked. Six days later, Iraq's General Kassem announced that Kuwait belonged to Iraq's Basra province and that Iraq's border would consequently be extended to the south of Kuwait. On June 30 Kuwait requested British assistance. By July 1 the British commando carrier *Bulwark* landed tanks and 600 marines. This contingent was quickly reinforced by some forty-five warships, including two aircraft carriers, and British forces in Kuwait grew to over 6,000.[4] Withdrawal began by July 7, but was not completed until October 19. The intelligence prompting this massive reaction, the reasons for Kuwait's delayed reaction in requesting British help, and Iraq's exact motivations are somewhat obscure.[5] Throughout, however, no shots were fired.

Iraq's claim to Kuwait was not new. The Kuwaiti Sheikhs' historical acceptance of Ottoman suzerainty gave Iraq, as the successor state from the Empire, at least the tenuous basis for a claim to Kuwaiti territory. One authority has suggested that Kassem's true motivation lay in "feverishly seeking some foreign issues with which to direct the attention of his disenchanted people from the sad state of domestic affairs."[6] Of at least equal importance to Iraq was the long-standing strategic priority of obtaining unthreatened control of a major Gulf port other than Basra with its vulnerabilities vis-à-vis the embittered Shatt al Arab dispute with Iran. Nuri es Said, prime minister of Iraq in its post-World War II Hashemite years, tried in 1954 to lure Kuwait into the Baghdad pact by offering to exchange full Kuwaiti access to the abundant water of the Shatt in return for Kuwait's Warbah Island. Warbah, opposite the larger Kuwaiti island of Bubiyan, sits astride the navigable route to Iraq's only alternative port, Um Qasr, which is less than a mile from Kuwait's disputed northern boundary. Warbah and/or Bubiyan in unfriendly hands could generate problems of free access to Um Qasr for Iraq reminiscent of the Shatt. Since one of General Kassem's early actions following the revolution in 1958 had been to borrow £66 million from the Soviets for port construction at Um Qasr, his motivation for acquisition of Kuwait's northern area was evident. Subsequent Iraqi governments have regularly applied pressure on Kuwait's frontier and asserted claims to Warbah and Bubiyan.

Whether Kassem ever intended to attack Kuwait remains unclear. He may merely have been testing Kuwaiti and world reaction or perhaps simply making a forceful record of reasserting an old Iraqi claim in the changed environment of full Kuwaiti independence. Obscurities abounded in the postmortem of the crisis. A little something for every viewpoint could be found. British critics of the operation charged the government with jingoism and military muscle flexing, in part to dissipate the still bitter aftertaste of Suez. Those favoring the expedition cited it as a model of planning and efficiency that deterred Kassem from his objective.

The principal lessons of the crisis, however, were far from obscure in their implications. First, Iraq possessed the only modernized Arab army in the entire Gulf area, a force that could have seized Kuwait in a matter of hours, virtually unopposed, had Kassem not given advance warning. Second, according to some military judgments, moreover, determined Iraqi opposition to the British landings might well have meant a disaster for British forces. Third, the rapid convergence of major British units was based on chance factors—HMS *Bulwark* happened to be visiting Karachi, the British tank brigade was afloat between Bahrain and Aden, and a planned NATO exercise off Portugal enabled the quick shifting of a landing group to Kuwait.

Although a small Arab League force of 1,400 Saudis, 800 Jordanians, and a few Sudanese and Egyptians eventually supplemented and replaced the British, the action displayed the weakness of the conservative Gulf countries' security system. The lesson was not lost, particularly on Saudi Arabia, as will be noted in more detail shortly. Demonstrably, the British operation was a far cry from the brief punitive expeditions or warning displays of the previous century and violated the standard dictum against incursions on land. The Indian soldiers, so vital in the past, were gone. British power was sharply diminished. Arab nationalism, even in the conservative states, found British intervention as unpalatable politically as did many British themselves. Yet force requirements arising from the introduction of modern Soviet weapons had nonetheless multiplied to an extent that the very massiveness of the British reaction appeared insufficient in pure military terms. All of this dramatized the need for a new security order in the Gulf.

Aden, by 1967, demonstrated even more salient implications for Gulf security. For most of the 150 years of British presence Aden Colony and the adjoining protectorates were ruled with fewer than 2,000 Indian and British troops, supplemented during much of the twentieth century by a few hundred Royal Air Force personnel. Paradoxically, the major build-up of forces at Aden did not begin until the colonial era entered its final stages. Forces were moved to Aden from Suez after the 1956 debacle, and by 1960 Aden had become headquarters of the British Middle East Command. Additional troops were moved to Aden from Kenya in 1964, bringing the total to over 8,000, excluding dependents.[7] Yet even these expanded numbers were inadequate. British political and military policies appeared to be on divergent tracks. Aden's political underpinnings had long been eroding. By 1964 they had reached the stage where the addition of new forces and the facilities to accommodate them merely added to the tensions propelling the situation toward the final embattled withdrawal. The last British troops were helicoptered from the colony to a naval task force on November 29, 1967.

Aden's utility as a base depended on its port bunkering facilities and airfield, which in turn were ultimately hostage to the colony's large labor force. Since 1948 and particularly from 1956, this labor force had been a source of recurrent unrest and strikes, many of which paralyzed the port. The republican revolution in North Yemen in 1962 brought Egyptian intrigues into the Aden protectorates along with smuggled weapons and an increased nationalist fever in the colony itself. By 1964 the bulk of British forces from the colony were tied down in the Radfan mountains suppressing an insurrection. The large North Yemeni population in the colony constituted an increasingly dangerous faction within a wider Arab nationalist impetus favoring the unity of North Yemen, the Western Protectorate, and Aden Colony. The continuing British efforts to federate the colony and parts of the protectorates further aroused nationalist resentments.

British military forces became so beleaguered that their presence lost its original purpose. Instead of bolstering British security interests in the area the military presence at Aden became a weakening factor as conservative states like Saudi Arabia and Kuwait increasingly shared the radical Arab states' objections to British activities in Aden Colony and the protectorates. The now counterproductive military tail at Aden was wagging the larger dog of British interests in the Gulf and beyond.

The Aden example therefore became profoundly influential in the debate over British security policy in the Gulf. Conservatives in Parliament, along with some in the Gulf itself as we shall note shortly, cited the collapsed federation effort and the ensuing Marxist-led takeover of Aden's and the protectorates' government as a bellwether of any British military withdrawal from the Gulf. Labourites, on the other hand, saw the forced evacuation beginning a trend that could only be stemmed by leaving the Gulf before nationalist and radical movements there, too, became entrenched and inflamed. Although the analogy between circumstances in Aden and the Gulf might be thin, there was sufficient parallelism for the episode to obtrude forcefully against the tendency of British Gulf policy to drift.

Changing Ideologies and Power

The sweep of Nasserism, of course, had opened the door for Soviet influence in the entire Middle East, adding to conditions unanticipated in the earlier British design of a security apparatus for the Gulf and the Arabian Peninsula area. By 1966, more than 60,000 Soviet-equipped Egyptian troops were engaged in the Yemeni civil war. When the 1967 Arab-Israeli war forced the withdrawal of these troops, Soviet direct aid to Yemen increased dramatically—with an emergency airlift and delivery of 24 fighter aircraft to the Yemeni republican forces. Nasser's planes bombed Saudi border towns in Asir province in late 1962.[8] Throughout the Gulf area, as elsewhere, Soviet opportunism pounced wherever there was an opening. Soviet success obviously came from riding with the waves of new nationalism. Against this force, a British security system designed to control nationalist elements became largely impotent. New Gulf forces were evolving, both military and political, however, that could join with Western interests to work toward another approach to Gulf defense.

Iran's steadily increasing economic and military power since World War II alone argued for a different regional role for that nation. The development of Saudi Arabian oil resources and the post-World War II impetus to national unity given by King Faisal similarly caused the old British Gulf role and treaties to appear increasingly anomalous. Activist

Iraq's role could only be countered by the kind of indigenous energy marshalled through a new order of political cooperation. Disputes needed to be settled by local forces and not by inevitably escalating Western or Soviet intervention. The viability of this process had already been demonstrated, clearly with British and U.S. encouragement, in November 1962 when Saudi Arabia established a joint defense council with Jordan to guard against further attacks on Saudi territory by Yemen's republican forces supported by the United Arab Republic.[9] The local and international political as well as military influences had become too strong and diverse for diminishing British power. British forces had been shown ineffective for the kinds of activities inherent in their original mission: they could not materially influence events when Mossadeq shut the oil valves in 1951, when Middle Eastern oil flow ceased in 1956 and 1967, or when oil negotiations in Teheran threatened Western interests in 1971.

The View from the West

Hardly was there British unanimity on the subject of their role in the Gulf. As early as 1959 a British authority anticipated that for Gulf security,

The real danger comes from without, not from Middle Eastern neighbors, but from doctrinaire politicians in the West . . . who think that, because democracy suits the West, it is a panacea for all ills in the East, and that any remaining vestiges of imperialism should, as such, be incontinently swept away. Such doctrines could lead to the premature abandonment by Great Britain of her position in the Gulf States with disastrous results both to the states themselves and to the oil companies whose operations have brought much benefit both to these states and to the Western world.[10]

Others identified growing contradictions between Britain's old imperial role and her new encouragement for Gulf national development that implied full independence for the states of the region. The transfer of British troops from Aden to Bahrain was said to "heighten a situation which should be compulsory study for students of the bizarre" wherein British troops were maintained in the Gulf "in order to prevent other countries shooting at each other with arms bought from Britain or the

United States."[11] Increasingly, recognition grew throughout the Arab world and in Britain that the "final remnant of British Raj," the Trucial system, "has been for some years now an obvious, if in some ways charming, anachronism."[12]

For the most part, however, both British and U.S. public assessments of the probable consequences of the military withdrawal from the Gulf were pessimistic, notwithstanding frequent acceptance of the motivating financial and political realities behind the decision. Senate Democratic Leader Mike Mansfield, despite State Department disavowal of plans to replace the British in the Gulf, said on January 17, 1968, "I am sorry the British felt they were forced to take this step because I am certain we will be asked to fill the vacuum east of Suez. I don't know how we are going to do it because I don't think we have the men or resources for it."[13] This fear of potential American involvement was echoed editorially by the *Washington Star* in the same issue carrying Mansfield's statement: "[Withdrawal] cannot fail to create a vacuum of power and unsettle the military balance in the areas affected."

These generally dire predictions affected America's capacity to accept even a cautious security role in the Gulf. Predictions emphasized the lurid, exaggerated the depth of historical enmities, and portrayed the entire area as chronically unstable. This tone of analysis by the media, by politicians, and by many academics derived partly from the politicized British debate over withdrawal in which each side heavily exaggerated its case. Moreover, the Gulf's combination of strategic resources, variety of traditional rulers, and color of history tempted even serious writers to glibness. In a special report published in 1969, Georgetown University's Center for Strategic and International Studies defined the Gulf as "a region of inherent instability . . . [where] the British have held tribal animosities in check . . . [and where] their withdrawal may well release traditional feuds and conflicting territorial claims among neighboring states."[14] The report further cited a "precarious" political order that is "vulnerable to seething pressures of Arab nationalism . . . [as well as] tribal dissidence, differences between Persians and Arabs . . . [and between] the two main Islamic sects."[15] The assessment classified Saudi Arabia as a "vast and ungainly land [which] . . . is not a natural unit either politically or geographically."[16]

The normally sober *Economist*, long after the initial excitement of British withdrawal, wrote in its May 1975 "Survey of the Gulf," "In political terms the ten [Gulf countries] . . . consist of one serious emerging power, Iran, two places that have to be taken into account, Iraq and Saudi Arabia, and seven peripheral curiosities, obscurities and nuisances [the latter being generally South Yemen]."

Not surprisingly, there was little public understanding of the actual Gulf situation. But pessimism prior to British military withdrawal was not limited to Western observers. The Shah of Iran suggested that "in light of Britain's experience in South Arabia, Nigeria and Rhodesia" sufficient evidence had accumulated to show that "tribalism and federalism were incompatible and the Persian Gulf federation would go the way of Aden and South Arabia."[17] The concept of an inherent Iranian-Saudi competition, which became the conventional wisdom of the early 1970s, was to some extent fed by the Shah's public comments. These comments often reflected a low opinion of the character and stability of the Arab regimes, undoubtedly evidencing the Shah's true view, but were also a device used to justify his rationale for Iran's preeminent Gulf role. The theme, in any event, persisted. Doomsayers clung to the notion of the development of a dangerous Saudi-Iranian competition easily exploited by the Soviets. The removal of what literally for more than 150 years had been the region's security blanket, the British security agreements and military presence, was thought "tantamount to a diplomatic and strategic revolution; and the fact that it is accompanied by equally radical economic, social, and political changes within the Gulf territories themselves as a consequence of soaring oil wealth and burgeoning nationalism only multiplies the uncertainties and tensions which it must release throughout the region."[18] In short, this authority concluded just before withdrawal that ". . . the Gulf must be regarded as on the brink of a period of upheaval greater than anything it has known since the British Raj took it under its capacious wing."[19]

CHAPTER THREE

Reality Versus Prediction

The Gulf's extraordinary progress in resolving old disputes, a process that strikingly contradicted prevailing pessimistic assessments, actually began with the prospect rather than the advent of British withdrawal. Iran and Saudi Arabia initiated a statesmanlike momentum in October 1968 when they resolved their highly complex and longstanding disagreement over the continental shelf in the Gulf. The issue had involved overlapping exploration and exploitation concessions on the seabed, and two disputed Gulf islands. Under the agreement, Iran obtained the island of Farsi and Saudi Arabia the island of al Arabi. Although little noticed, this agreement, according to one authority, provided "an imaginative solution . . . [which] meant that Iran and Saudi Arabia had decided to share, in effect, an enormous seabed oil resource in the Persian Gulf."[1] Clearly, both countries, undoubtedly with British encouragement, acted from a sense of urgency to create a cooperative atmosphere in advance of actual British withdrawal. The alternative might well have meant the engagement of passions in the larger Arab world through which the Soviets could have exerted political leverage. But momentum of statesmanship had begun and by June 1969 Iran and Qatar signed a similar agreement demarcating marine areas between them.[2]

A more pointedly dangerous issue for Gulf stability had been Iran's claim to Bahrain based on Nadir Shah's seizure of the island in 1937 as he gained conrol of the Gulf.[3] A small percentage of Bahrain's non-Arab population, which represents about 15 percent of the island's total, is Iranian. Dangerous for Gulf stability as Iran's claim was, however, there is little to suggest that the Shah ever intended to cloud the entire spectrum of Iran's relationships with the Arab world by forcing the issue. His claim fitted within a complex bargaining process coinciding with British military withdrawal. Fearful of chaotic conditions in the Gulf on the heels of British departure, he opposed federation of the lower Gulf states and retained his claim to Bahrain until his own conditions were met. As one authority points out, the Shah's claim to Bahrain was made "to bargain with the British for the establishment of Iranian forces on three other islands in the Gulf, which Iran also claimed."[4]

Intensive mediation by Saudi Arabia during meetings in 1968 and 1969 between Iran, Saudi Arabia, Kuwait, and Bahrain led to Iran's agreement to give up its claims to Bahrain. The Shah's visits to Saudi Arabia and Kuwait during November 1968 evidenced the diplomatic process underway. The Shah's dramatic anouncement on January 4, 1969 that Iran would withdraw its claim to Bahrain should "the people of Bahrain . . . not want to join my country" was followed by the mission to Bahrain in 1970 by the U.N. Secretary General's representative, who subsequently confirmed Bahrain's desire for independence.[5] The Shah had obviously recognized that Bahrain's predominantly Arab population would not desire incorporation into Iran, and having agreed to the mission he had in effect already relinquished his claim.

In the meantime the Shah had negotiated the occupation of Abu Musa Island with the British and the Ruler of Sharjah. Abu Musa, together with the two Tunb islands, also in the Strait of Hormuz, could provide a hostile occupier, in the Shah's view, with easy means to block the narrow strait through which Iran's oil moves to market. Long negotiations between Britain, Iran, and the Sheikh of Ras al Khaimah failed to culminate in agreement and the Shah's forces occupied the Tunbs regardless, virtually coincident with British withdrawal. His negotiated occupation of Abu Musa provided for economic assistance included in a memorandum of understanding between Abu Musa, Iran, and Britain. Publicity surrounding the occupation of these islands overlooked the diplomatic background and generated temporary furor in parts of the Arab world. Iran's accumulated propaganda and diplomatic credit on the Bahrain and federation issues, however, amply offset this criticism.

The Momentum of Healing: Buraimi Oases

Fixed land boundaries throughout the Gulf were historically unknown and would have been irrelevant to tribal practices.[6] But usage of grazing land and water long formed the basis for warfare among competing tribes. One of the most notable of these disputes, among Saudi Arabia, Abu Dhabi, and Oman, exemplified the potential for eruption that so fixated many Gulf watchers. The area at issue was huge, as shown by the Saudi note of 1949 to the British claiming "sovereignty over the greater part of the territory lying between the base of the Qatar peninsula and the southeastern corner of the Persian Gulf."[7] Four-fifths of Abu Dhabi was encompassed by the claim, including the home oasis of the ruling family of Abu Dhabi. The issue had not only divided key Gulf countries but had embittered Saudi relations with the British, who sided with the Sultanate of Muscat and Oman by virtue of treaty obligations, apart from any other motivations. After a stage of physical confrontation in 1952, a standstill agreement was reached and the dispute moved to international arbitration in 1954. The Saudi claim was described in the monumental three-volume *Saudi Memorial of 1955*. The 1956 Saudi-British agreement for direct discussions was ruptured by the 1956 debacle in Suez, and it was not until 1963 that the two countries restored diplomatic relations.

The issue remained in dispute, according to one authority, less on the basis of territory than as "the outgrowth of a clash between the strong personalities of two men, Shaykh Zayd and King Faysal."[8] But the problems were also unquestionably substantive, involving oil resources both in being and potential, as well as the importance of the oases to Abu Dhabi as a primary fresh water source. Despite the force of emotions and complexity of claims, however, wise leadership again prevailed. In 1974 Saudi Arabia and Abu Dhabi signed two agreements settling their boundaries and providing Saudi recognition of the United Arab Emirates, whose capital is Abu Dhabi, as well as Saudi renunciation of claims to the oases.

Back from the Brink: Iran and Iraq

The most actively hostile and therefore potentially threatening Gulf disputes were between Iran and Iraq. Both countries, with justification, attached vital issues of national survival to their claims. Ideology greatly widened the gap. A radical Baathist, pro-Marxist Iraq politically and militarily supported by the Soviets confronted a monarchical and capitalist Iran closely allied with the United States.

Toward its final stages during 1975, Iran's direct support of the

Kurdish rebellion in Iraq's north, that had long drained Iraq's military and financial resources, escalated to the level of open Iranian artillery barrages across the Iraqi frontier. Iraq, in turn, applied pressure on the many Iranians of Shia faith living in Iraq, particularly in the important Shia shrine cities of Karbala and Najaf. Iraq also retaliated by reiteration of its claim to Iran's Khuzistan province, by radio propaganda beamed into Iran, and by training and other direct support to Iranian terrorists.

As if these apparently intractable conflicts were not sufficient, the two countries remained locked in opposition over the issue of their boundary along the Shatt al Arab (the combined flow of the Tigris and Euphrates rivers that empties into the Persian Gulf). Iraq had refused to negotiate from the treaty of 1937, which was supposed to form the beginning of a joint commission to establish details for use of the waterway. Iran was stuck with its critical ports and facilities at Khorramshahr and Abadan (with the exception of two small sections directly opposite these ports) potentially throttled by a boundary running along the low water mark on Iran's side rather than along the main navigation channel, or thalweg.[9] In effect, Iranian ships had to pass through Iraqi-claimed waters for 40 miles to reach Iran's key ports. Negotiations were stonewalled by Iraq, and by all appearances the issue seemed likely to remain deadlocked. With the Kurdish problem, these issues continued to bear the potential for a major conflict easily spreading to involve other Arab states against Iran, or superpower confrontation. All of these impediments notwithstanding, Iran and Iraq, in a uniquely swift burst of diplomacy, announced settlement on March 6, 1975 of all outstanding issues between them. The joint statement came from Algiers where President Boumedienne's mediation apparently had proved instrumental. Both countries accepted the thalweg principle for the Shatt al Arab, and Iran agreed to cease support for the Kurdish insurgents who were given the option of immigrating to Iran or receiving amnesty in Iraq. While no analyst could assume from this settlement the dawning of perpetual brotherhood and peace between the two deeply antagonistic states, the magnitude of the diplomatic achievement and its subsequent staying power are stunning.

Cooperation Tested: The Dhofar Rebellion

Insurgency in the Dhofar province of Oman, a dispute of a different kind, emerged by 1972, in the opinion of responsible authorities, as a "struggle . . . [which] may well signal the beginning of a longterm threat to Western oil supplies."[10] In fact, they suggested that "a comparison between the war in Dhofar and Vietnam is illuminating and by no means farfetched."[11] The insurgency in its modern form was led, since the mid-1960s, by the Dhofar Liberation Front, whose inspiration was a mix of nationalism, Marxism, and Nasserism. As the British were forced out in late 1967, Aden became independent, and the Marxist-controlled National Liberation Front came to power in what was now to be called the Peoples' Democratic Republic of South Yemen (PDRY). The PDRY extended increasing material and political support to the Front, whose greatly expanded aims were expressed in the new title, The Popular Front for the Liberation of the Occupied Arab Gulf (PFLOAG).

The ingredients for a wider war gathered as the PDRY obtained Soviet, Cuban, East German, and, for a time, Chinese advisors and military equipment and training for the insurgents. PFLOAG leaders were trained in Odessa, Peking, and Iraq. The Sultan of Oman, on the other hand, continued to receive British assistance for training his forces and developing a small air force. As many as 80 British officers served at one time, on loan from the British army or as retirees on direct contract to the sultanate. Further, many of the sultan's forces were comprised of Baluchis, Pakistanis, and Indians. The insurgency dragged on, although estimates of the actual number of militarily active Dhofaris ranged only from 700 to 1,000. As a result, British political sensitivities mounted over the combat exposure of personnel and to occasional accusations that the rebellion was deliberately allowed to fester so as to prolong British influence in Oman. Extremely rugged and mountainous terrain covered thickly by vegetation during part of the year complicated the sultan's efforts.

Dhofari motivations were lodged sufficiently deep in history to have sustained the rebellion even without the overlay of Marxist and Maoist indoctrination provided by the PDRY. Long possessed with a different sense of identity from the ruling tribes of Muscat and Oman, the Dhofari had not only rebelled many times before, but in 1896 had also caused the British, through the government of India, to help the Sultan of Muscat with "two mortars and ammunition as an addition to his means of defense, and an offer of naval assistance for the purpose of recovering the province of Dhufar, which had revolted."[12] The stubbornness of the rebellion finally provoked a response from Jordan, which, undoubtedly with Saudi encouragement, sent an engineering batallion to support the sultan's counterinsurgency effort. The crucial outside assistance, however, came from Iran, which by December 1973 at the sultan's request sent a battle group of 1,200 to Dhofar to bolster the sultan's British-led forces; by 1975 this was expanded to 2,000, including air support. Saudi and UAE financial aid were also pivotal.[13] Coupled with the sultan's and the Britishers' skill in developing economic inducements to settle the rebels, the addition of Iranian forces applied sufficient added pressure that by 1976 the rebellion virtually collapsed. By mid-1977 only a handful of Iranian army specialists remained in Oman, an evolution that disproved those doubters who had initially feared that Iran's interest in the Dhofar campaign represented the beginning of a permanent Iranian military foothold on the Arab side of the Gulf.

This example of Iranian-Arab cooperation has profound significance. While Saudi Arabia clearly would have preferred to have been the intervening power, and undoubtedly viewed Iranian actions with mixed envy and concern, the fact remains that, instead of the Iranian-Arab tension and hostility that was to have so seriously jeopardized Gulf stability, a successful joint military campaign was mounted against what was clearly recognized as a common threat.[14] Oman's somewhat isolated and unique status within the Arab world does not detract from the new impetus of cooperation in the Gulf that the successful Iranian intervention represented. Earlier examples of a Saudi Arabian and Iranian confluence of military interests should not be overlooked. Both countries cooperated in supporting Yemeni royalists during the 1962–1968 civil war and Iran loaned military equipment to Saudi Arabia in 1969 when the PDRY was violating the Saudi border.

Certainly, Gulf problems remain. Iraq's claims to parts of Kuwait, particularly the Bubiyan and Warbah islands as already noted, remain a source of periodic tension in the Gulf, although the two countries agreed in July 1977 to partial withdrawal of forces from the disputed border areas and to formation of a joint committee to strive for a settlement. Familial disputes between rulers are always potentially explosive, such as between Bahrain and Qatar, and Abu Dhabi and Dubai. The close family ties between the rulers of Qatar and Dubai are an undoubted worry for the ruling family of Bahrain. Overall, however, cooperation in the Gulf has blossomed far beyond the expectations of even the most optimistic observers who made predictions about Gulf events shortly before or after British withdrawal. The question remains as to why most predictions were so wide of the mark.

CHAPTER FOUR

Why the Clouded Lens

The Mist of Thin Analogies

In simple terms, predictions about Gulf events based primarily on past Gulf behavior often neglected to recognize the force of modern influences. Many predictions were made, of course, before Gulf oil income quadrupled in 1973 and before substantial new oil discoveries in several of the United Arab Emirates. Obviously, as the size of the area's income pie increased dramatically the incentive soared to put aside or compromise on ancient disputes that could otherwise disrupt the flow of income. Many disputes, as noted earlier, derived from the paucity of Gulf resources. Although some resources, such as natural water, had become even scarcer in relation to population, technology and available money opened the way for development of alternative supplies.

More important, the continued British presence as arbiter, and particularly as representative of the interests of the smaller Gulf states, tended to perpetuate rather than solve old arguments. British diplomacy in the Gulf was brilliant prior to withdrawal and eased formation of the United Arab Emirates. But in other critical problem areas, their very presence brought into play the interests of a third party with a long colonial past and a NATO and CENTO membership. Complex disputes were therefore further encumbered by the presence of real or imagined British interests, not only heavy with history, but further weighted with superpower connotations. Minus the British, the UAE could deal with Saudi Arabia on the Buraimi dispute with one entire set of psychological subissues out of the way. Iran could settle its foremost problems with Iraq minus the presence of British forces and security commitments in the Gulf that strongly influenced both the political and military equation. In short, contrary to so many predictions, rather than constituting

24   THE CLOUDED LENS

the indispensable force for Gulf stability, the British military presence
had reached the point of diminishing returns, where its departure
meant a net gain for Gulf stability.

An additional miscalculation arose as most prognoses for the Gulf
were based on conventional (and for the most part usually valid elsewhere) hypotheses regarding the need for tandem economic and
political development. In noting, however, that "in most Gulf states a
restless, educated middle class—largely drawn from other Arab countries—carries the germ of rising expectations, reform, or 'revolution,' "
too many observers extrapolated overly from the urban experience of
the wider Middle East.[1] Only Kuwait, Bahrain, and Iran can be said to
have a component of society definable as a restless middle class. The
estimated 200,000 Palestinians in Kuwait represent a potentially destabilizing force even though many have been absorbed into important
decision-making positions. Iran, with a large indigenous urban middle
class, is a special case, but it is doubtful whether the expatriate employees
and workers who have poured into the Gulf from other Arab and non-
Arab countries for the sake of lucrative jobs now constitute a menacing
political infestation. Yet many authorities disagree. Bill and Leiden
wrote in 1974 that "the chances for explosive unrest and violent upheaval increase as the gap between level of modernization and level of
political development enlarges" and "the most potentially volatile part of
the Middle East is the Persian Gulf area," where, "in the Sheikhdoms,
petroleum discoveries have spurred dramatic modernization while political processes have changed little from medieval times."[2] This probable misreading overlooks the greater vulnerability of Iran, Bahrain,
and Kuwait.

But the social pressures of Cairo, Damascus, and Teheran are one
thing, and those of Jidda, Abu Dhabi, and Kuwait another. Most of the
Middle East countries have not experienced the almost explosive out-
pouring of wealth, jobs, and welfare unique to the Gulf. The Gulf countries do not share the recent historical memory of direct European
colonial rule and the consequent tendency to hate and distrust authority
of all kinds.[3] Nor were the Gulf countries traumatized politically by
direct defeat at the hands of Israeli forces in Palestine during 1948.
Finally, it is misleading to assert that "political processes have changed
little from medieval times"[4] in the Gulf sheikhdoms. As in Saudi Arabia
and Kuwait, the growth of bureaucracies and dependence on technical
expertise and planners even in the most autocratically administered

emirate bring change in the political process. Increasingly, technocrats widen their role in decision making, and as the complexity of the state increases the ruler finds his ability to freewheel inevitably subjected to a process of limitation by the administrative apparatus upon which he must depend for implementation of bold infrastructure modernization programs. As more and more people become involved in and knowledgeable of the workings of the state administration, the power of the ruler to do as he pleases must naturally diminish, at least in the kind of patriarchal Arab society to which we refer. Certainly, if the Saudi evolution is any guide to the future of the sheikhdoms, the rulers will have already discovered the inevitable diffusion of power occasioned by increasing urbanization and development programs. The process does not signal a sure march toward parliamentary democracy by any means. Rather, the inner political relationships are expanding.

For the emirates the very fact of federation changed the political processes, however slow the evolution to truly federal government. For the Gulf area as a whole, sharply increased resources coupled with the virtually universal decision to push ahead rapidly on all manner of development projects may mean in some cases even a slowing of the buildup of pressures for more representative forms of government. With all levels of skill in great demand for economic programs, and education freely available, the most likely sources of discontent in many cases appear at least temporarily co-opted.

British Rule Misread

Many observers were also misled both by their conception of the actual British military presence that departed in late 1971 and by their misreading of the extent of continuity of the British internal security effort following departure. Throughout the Gulf the British for many years had assisted the development of local armed forces for internal security. Until the 1956 riots in Bahrain, the British Gulf command was limited to a few support personnel, and it was not until British units were transferred from Aden to the Gulf in 1967 that a modern force capable of repelling any determined external threat was stationed in the Gulf. The joint task force headquartered at Bahrain at the time of withdrawal included 9,000 men, divided between Sharjah and Bahrain. About 4,700 of these were army. The 3,400-man Royal Air Force operated one jet fighter squadron from Sharjah and one from Bahrain. The Royal Navy component included three destroyer escorts, each with a small Royal Marine force supported by a helicopter, and six coastal minesweepers.[5] As previously noted, the considerable British military presence in Oman was not affected by withdrawal. Iran, Saudi Arabia, and Kuwait, of course, had long been in the process of developing local forces of their own.

Conscious of the vulnerability of the sheikhdoms to political subversion, from Iraq and the PDRY particularly, the British made careful efforts to assure at least temporary continuity of the intelligence and countersubversion units that had been developed over many years under their special treaty relationships. British-led special branch units were left functioning in Bahrain, Qatar, and in the sheikhdoms. Many of these British cadres naturally have been phased out, but apparently effective structures remain, and, most important, the particularly vulnerable early stages following British withdrawal passed successfully. One of the most important contributions of these cadres was implementing the communications on security matters between Gulf states. Virtually all of the Gulf rulers saw this as essential following British departure. Therefore, in early capacity to cope with both military and internal threats, even the small Gulf states, while far from robustly equipped, were left with a functioning structure quite in contrast to the popular image of an area stripped naked by the withdrawal of the forces presumed to have ·had a far more direct role in Gulf affairs than had ever been the case.

The Paradox of Post-Withdrawal Security

But what would replace that British role which kept major military crises from erupting, or prevented powers external to the Gulf from intervening militarily in times of crisis? In fact, a psychological restraint became manifest, perhaps as powerful as the previous pervasive influence of potential British military intervention. By 1972, and particularly after 1973, every Gulf area leader, no matter how supposedly unsophisticated or medieval, came to realize that any substantial conflict in the Gulf would bring outside intervention as inevitably as during the British era. The Gulf, in one paradoxical sense, passed into a more urgently interpreted security framework than the previous pleasantly anachronistic system had provided. Saudi interests, for instance, could not tolerate a significant military encroachment in the Gulf by Iran. Should Iran so err, however, much of the Arab world, including Egypt, Jordan, Syria, and undoubtedly Iraq, would mobilize for economic as well as nationalistic reasons to a degree Iran would be incapable of withstanding, financially or militarily. As if this were not sufficient deterrence, Iran would also confront the Saudi/U.S. special relationship and its own special relationship with the U.S., including the requirement for U.S. logistics to support any sustained military operation.

In turn, Iran, if threatened beyond the point of acceptance, aside from application of locally superior military force, would assuredly invoke long-standing U.S. expressions of support for Iran's security. In extremis, it is certainly not out of the question that Iran, too, might precipitously expand ties with the Soviets or even the Israelis, whose military skill and mobility is acutely understood throughout the Gulf area. Gone are the romantic days of tribal disputes, erupting personal feuds between rulers, and wars over undefined boundaries. Such disruptions are a luxury the Gulf knows it cannot afford as a primary fuel source for Western Europe, Japan, and increasingly, the United States. With NATO strength ultimately dependent on its oil, the Gulf has become strategic in superpower competition.

Beyond these factors, which have speeded the trend of accommodation in the Gulf, there are two additional influences so obvious they are often overlooked. First, while the authoritarian nature of the Gulf political systems poses obvious risks, the attendant capacity for decisive diplomatic action gives the leader of each country great flexibility. Absent is the requirement to engage in the arduous processes that surround, for example, the U.S. president in arranging a Panama Canal treaty or the prime minister of Israel in marshaling the multiparty consensus that would enable negotiations over the West Bank. Whether the disputes will stay settled is another matter, but their early resolution has bought valuable time for the nascent phase of the evolving Gulf system of political stability and therefore for Western security interests.

Second, Soviet influence in most of the Middle East, including to a degree the radical Arab states of the PDRY and Iraq, has steadily eroded since 1972. Nor has another Nasser arisen to inflame passions and ripen the political atmosphere in which subversive cells incubate. Neither Iraq, the PDRY, Somalia nor, least of all, Egypt, where the Soviets labored to create attractive models for their cause, easily capture the imaginations of potential revolutionaries in the Gulf area. How long this quiescence will continue as a major trend is uncertain, but the Gulf's period of grace is shared with Western security interests.

CHAPTER FIVE

Evolving Security Concepts

Following the announcement of intended British withdrawal in 1968, the theoretically most useful step on behalf of collective security for the Gulf area would have been the careful creation of a Gulf security pact.[1] Such a pact or treaty would have defined various threats, assigned force levels or force development goals for each state, and perhaps even provided for a joint defense command. Economies in scarce manpower allocations for military purposes could have been accomplished, to say nothing of financial savings, and most important, of course, would have been the decreased opportunity for hostile forces to intervene either militarily or by subversion.

Toward Quiet Alliances

In the absence of the necessary political underpinning, however, formal security agreements remained and still remain in the realm of pure theorizing. Clearly, any formal defense alliance between states must be preceded by solid political agreements and a sufficient logic of force balance between the states to provide each with a clear mission. None of these conditions was present in the Gulf in 1968 and none has yet been fully realized since. As already noted, the major process of settling disputes did not gain full momentum until after British forces departed, although British efforts were instrumental as early as 1922 when the neutral zone between Kuwait and Saudi Arabia was created. Iran's military development long exceeded that of any other Gulf power with the exception of Iraq. But because of the wide ideological schism between Iraq and Saudi Arabia, not to mention Iran's virtual state of undeclared war with Iraq, Iraq could in no way assume a balancing role vis-à-vis Iran on behalf of the Gulf's Arab states. Iran's increasingly open support for the Kurdish rebellion in Iraq compounded the impediments to formal Iranian-Arab alliances, especially as active Israeli assistance to the Iraqi Kurds created a tacit Iranian-Israeli joint paramilitary effort. Moreover, the emirates, although formally established on December 2, 1971 (with the exception of Ras al Khaimah, which did not join until February 10, 1972), could hardly have been expected to join an external alliance during the period when they were laboring to achieve a viable union.

Attempts to accelerate artificially the processes of history were doomed to failure, particularly if fostered by a power external to the Gulf. British diplomatic activity was intense throughout the Gulf, including Iran, where Minister of State Goronwy Roberts made several visits during late 1967 and early 1968. This coincided with Iran's "formal expression of willingness to join Arab countries in defending the Persian Gulf."[2] The Iranian offer was met with a resounding Arab silence. On January 29, 1968 Undersecretary of State Eugene Rostow's statement on the Voice of America that, "the United States relied on the security grouping involving Turkey, Iran, Pakistan, Kuwait and Saudi Arabia to fill the vacuum left by Britain's withdrawal from the Gulf,"[3] provoked a strongly negative attack against Western-sponsored pacts in Damascus, Bahgdad, and Cairo, as well as less vociferous but equally negative reaction from Riyadh. The same negativism had been stirred during the preceding week by reports that the British minister of state for foreign affairs had proposed a joint defense arrangement to the Shah. Regional objections were echoed by the Soviets in March 1968 when Tass opposed British and U.S. efforts to "palm off plans to make Iran, Turkey, Pakistan, Iraq, Arabia, and Kuwait the core of the new block."[4] A similar Iranian effort was rebuffed in June 1969. The Shah said, "We would be willing, in conjunction with Saudi Arabia, to pro-vide protection to the Gulf states," noting that "our paratroop and armoured regiments at Shiraz can give them as much protection as the British forces in the area today which would probably not fight anyway if the situation became serious."[5]

A pattern had emerged. Just as the Arab Gulf states did not want to be drawn into superpower disputes by joining superpower-linked alliances, they did not want to join and exacerbate each others' quarrels. This was evidenced by failure of the July 1970 Iraqi proposal for an Arab defense organization, which showed "an . . . inability to appreciate the smaller states' reluctance to become entangled in Iraqi-Iranian disputes."[6] Iran, after all, was still a CENTO country, and, however much the Shah may deride the impotence of the organization in military terms, CENTO symbolism in Arab eyes remained a factor. Iran's special relationship with Israel can, on the Arab side of the Gulf, raise the question whether shared Gulf intelligence and planning might be passed from Teheran to Tel Aviv. Moreover, any formal alliance or security pact with Iran could have been construed as endorsing various Iranian claims rejected by the Arab states.

Military Prerequisites for Stability: Iran

The Shah, expressing characteristic lack of confidence in U.S. responsiveness to what he regarded as Pakistan's legitimate claims for support under its bilateral and CENTO treaties, in 1975 reiterated, "We cannot rely on others for our defense; that is why we are brushing up our own forces."[7] The Shah occasionally indulges the luxury of his close U.S. ties to rail against U.S. unreliability to allies. This becomes a stimulus and additional justification for Iranian military self-sufficiency. As we shall note below, however, one of the ironies for developing nations is that pursuing the will-o'-the-wisp of self-sufficiency entails protracted dependence on the supplier of advanced weaponry.

The Shah, appreciating his ultimate dependence on U.S. political and military backing against the Soviets, had every reason to make a virtue of necessity. Noting the Vietnam backwash in the U.S. coupled with a sharp decline in British power, he was quick to capitalize on the useful harmony between his own goal of greater independence, power, and influence and the West's declining willingness and, in some cases, ability to act forcefully on behalf of regional allies. The Shah's approach to Iranian national security is not mincing. He asks, "What is the use of having an advanced industry in a country which could be brought to its knees when faced with any small, asinine event? . . . There is no economic power without military power."[8]

We have noted how earlier Gulf history was influenced by foreign military power exercised on a small but decisive scale. By the time of British withdrawal, Iran and Iraq had long before made their decisions to develop modern military forces, as had Saudi Arabia, albeit on a more modest scale. Clearly, the first prerequisite for a Gulf security system was the development of credible defense forces on both sides of the Gulf. That there should have been an increased sense of urgency attached to these efforts as withdrawal took place reflects logical analysis rather than the bizarre, menacing, and unnatural phenomenon identified by some observers. Iran obviously felt threatened in the broadest sense, not only by the all-too-fresh memory of Soviet occupation and pressure, but by the recent stridency of Nasserism, the pressures generated by the 1958 revolution and Soviet influence in Iraq, and uncertain degrees of stability in neighboring Pakistan and Afghanistan. The military coup in Afghanistan during late April 1978, which brought to power Noor Mohammad Taraki, a leader of the Afghan Communist Party, can only have confirmed the Shah's commitment.

Much speculation has centered on Iran's rationale for developing a modern naval force. Yet we should recall that "starting with the Dutch attack on Qishm Island in the 17th century, and continuing with Britain's occupation of Kharg Island (1838–1842, 1852–1857) and Britain's periodic naval pressure, inter alia in 1888, 1932, and 1951, Iran remained exposed to states possessing superior naval power."[9] Iran's more current concerns, as described earlier, focused on Iraq, whose successful threat in 1961 to block ships flying Iran's flag from passing through waters claimed by Iraq was a motivating factor behind Iran's naval development. In 1969 this development proved sufficient to deter Iraq from acting on a renewal of the threat, as "Iranian warships escort[ed] an Iranian merchant ship from Khorramshahr to the Persian Gulf in defiance of an Iraqi threat. . . ."[10] Iran's deep water Kharg Island terminal, however, is still only slightly over 100 miles from Iraq, Iranian offshore oil rigs are highly vulnerable in the Gulf, and the vital Abadan refinery is within mortar range of the Iraqi border.

Considering Iraqi statements in the U.N. during both 1969 and 1970, it was not surprising when Iran's foreign minister, explaining an increase in Iran's defense budget in February 1970, said, "We have no alternative but to resort to defense measures when the Iraqi delegate to the U.N. claims that Iran is an alien power in the Persian Gulf."[11] Iraq, with only a third of Iran's population, has consistently supported general equivalency with Iran in major weapons. It introduced into the Gulf area the first supersonic fighter aircraft—the MiG–15 and MiG–17—in 1958, and the first medium-range surface-to-surface missiles—the Styx and Frog—in 1973.

Considerable Iraqi combat experience, both against Israel and during the protracted Kurdish rebellion, must also be included in the equation. Even the July 1976 Staff Report to the Subcommittee on Foreign Assistance of the Senate Committee on Foreign Relations, entitled "U.S. Military Sales to Iran," stated "the military threats to Iran's security seem to be sufficiently real and diverse to enable the Shah to justify major investments in military forces. . . . In short, it is difficult to criticize Iran's perception that it needs a modern military force."[12] This report, both in the timing of its release just prior to presidential elections and in its content, can hardly be classified as a nonpolitical document. The publication helped illuminate arms sales into a campaign issue with particular criticism of the Nixon and Ford administrations' sales policies to Iran.

During the late 1950s and throughout much of the 1960s, Iran was confronted by Arab claims in which its "richest province of Khuzistan was called 'Arabistan' to emphasize the view that it was part of the Arab nation and that it had been lost to the Arab peoples as the result of British manipulation of Riza Sha."[13] Though the Arab world today, for the most part, enjoys a positive relationship with Iran, this issue remains latent. A poster by the Democratic Revolutionary Movement for the Liberation of Arabistan observed recently near the Libya Palace Hotel reads, "Support the Arabistan Peoples' Struggle." The province, of course, contains Iran's principal oil wells and ports.[14] A conference of Arab jurists in December 1964 claimed Khuzistan as "an integral part of the Arab Homeland, a claim supported by the Government of Syria in November 1965."[15] Of all countries, then, Iran, Muslim but of the heterodox Shia sect, in a sense culturally unique with a vast and vulnerable coastline, and with a land mass seven times the size of West Germany, has ample justification for developing modern military forces. While these forces could never halt a major Soviet thrust (a task left to the U.S.), they are rapidly developing the capability to block Soviet proxy military intervention, as demonstrated in Oman.

Iran's security concepts have also evolved in response to the dramatic increase in India's military capabilities during the last decade and in relation to the altered strategic configuration on the subcontinent after the split of Pakistan into two countries in December 1971. Although the Pakistan that emerged is in many ways a more viable state than when linked with an eastern province, the manner in which the so-called dismemberment occurred, with Soviet backing of Indian military force, drew Iran closer to Pakistan. The subcontinent balance of power became altered. Without Iranian backing, Pakistan had become potentially vulnerable to its own separatist tendencies in the event of pressure from Afghanistan and/or India, both of whose ethnic compositions create particular capability for intervention. Pakistan's security therefore bears directly on Iran's. The two countries share the problem of secessionist aspirations among the Baluchi tribal peoples inhabiting their common border areas. While there have been consistent reports of Indian and Soviet meddling among the Pathan tribes of northern Pakistan and among the Baluchis in the south, the more lurid assessments of a carefully masterminded Soviet intrigue for a Soviet-dominated independent Baluchistan remain unsubstantiated. The potential for a separatist Pathan/Baluchi corridor from the Soviet Asian republics to the Arabian Sea nonetheless remains.

That the development of modern forces required extensive foreign training and advisory assistance merely meant continuity for Iran rather than innovation. As A. T. Wilson notes, "From the beginning of the 20th century it had been the established practice of the Persians to employ Europeans in positions of responsibility. . . . Swedish officers had been placed in charge of the gendarmerie in 1912."[16] Wilson also quotes a French officer born in Persia to the effect that Nadir Shah's army (1736–1747) "included Arabs, Kurds, Turkmans, Afghans and Indians," a device which "excited the emulation of the Persians who, being naturally proud and unable to suffer that their chief's success should be attributed other than to themselves, fought ten times better than if they had been alone."[17] Curzon, writing in 1892 with the romanticized paternalism so characteristic of the era, on the one hand said that "the Persian army, even at this day, exists only by virtue of what British officers did for it in the past," and on the other hand quoted Herodotus, who said, "Persians at Plataea were not one whit inferior to the Greeks in courage and warlike spirit."[18]

The army of Iran had then often consisted of a hodgepodge of foreign advisory personnel, including a corps of Russians who were captured in 1826 and then deserted Russia, in addition to other "relics of the successive waves of foreign military importation . . . [that] still survive in Persia in 1891 in the person of seven Austrian officers, six of whom are generals, and one major, a French bandmaster dignified with the rank of a general, an Italian and a Bulgarian chief of instructors, an Italian head of police and two Prussian officers, acting as professors in the Royal College . . ." all representing "the flotsam and jetsam that the receding tide of polyglot military influence has left stranded upon the dubious shore-line of Teheran."[19]

However mixed their origins in training, equipment, and doctrine, Iranian forces have inherited a base unique in the region. Regular training on the disciplined European model began in 1800, a form of conscription in 1842; by 1932 two military schools staffed by foreign-trained Persians were functioning in Teheran, and more than 100 officers were receiving training in France and Germany. At the same time, six Italian gunboats had been purchased and 100 officers and 50 sailors had been sent to Italy for training.[20]

As Iran absorbed U.S. and other nations' World War II weapons that came largely as a result of postwar Soviet pressures, and as Iran began to acquire more advanced weapons in the 1960s, principally in response to the presence of advanced Soviet weapons and training in Iraq, the need for Western military technicians and instructors mounted. Politically and strategically, Iran had long since made the decision to go it alone in defense, if necessary, albeit on the basis of having to endure the paradox of a protracted and substantial dependence on her supplier nations for expertise and spare parts. As Iranian use of advanced weaponry has grown so has her dependence on the U.S. for continued access to the fast-moving flow of military high technology and for strategic logistical support in the event of a lengthy major conflict. In the absence of these implied commitments from the U.S., the credibility of Iran's defense capability would quickly weaken, a point for later discussion.

Response to Military Challenges: Saudi Arabia

From Saudi Arabia's standpoint, British departure from the Gulf meant merely an acceleration of an existing policy to develop modern defense forces. Abdul Aziz Ibn Saud had founded modern Saudi Arabia by bringing justice and order to the almost entirely independent and often very powerful tribes of the Hejaz province. These tribes within their "own roaming area . . . behaved as absolute masters, compelling caravans—not excepting official caravans traveling with military escorts—to pay tolls."[21] Once having completed this unifying task, however, Saudi Arabia did not launch an effort to develop European-type forces until well after World War II. This was in part by choice, in part because of insufficient resources, and in part because potential weapons suppliers denied the necessary equipment.[22] The Saudi kingdom, consolidated in 1932, then allowed its tribal forces practically to disband. The U.S. began a small training effort for the Saudi air force in 1947 in return for establishment and use of a military airfield at Dhahran. At the same time, the British initiated a modest training program (one mechanized unit) for the Saudi army. This program was taken over by the U.S. Military Training Mission in 1952.

By the 1960s, however, the need for more substantial modern forces became increasingly evident. This need was vividly illustrated when the Saudis had to borrow ARAMCO trucks to transport troops for the defense of Kuwait against the 1961 Iraqi challenge. A Saudi High Defense Council was established in July 1964 for the purpose of framing a long-range defense policy. As King Faisal assumed leadership in 1964, Saudi Arabia, despite its largely defenseless posture, had been drawn into the North Yemen civil war. This war eventually brought over 60,000 Egyptian troops to Yemen, with Egyptian bombing raids on five Saudi border towns, and bombardment of a coastal village by three Egyptian destroyers.[23] Shortly thereafter, the Saudis invited a U.S. fighter-interceptor squadron from Europe to Riyadh for an aerial demonstration.

With the establishment of a joint Saudi-Jordanian military command, through the Taif Pact of August 30, 1962, relatively poorly equipped and trained Saudi troops served with far sharper Jordanian forces on the Yemen border. Saudi troops had also served at Aqaba in Jordan in 1957. The impact of the consequent embarrassment and ridicule within Saudi Arabia, a country with a proud military tradition, cannot be overestimated. The Saudi exposure to joint field service with far better equipped and trained forces reverberated back to the Saudi royal family through tribal leaders and the echelons of the armed forces. By 1965 the Saudis had placed orders for U.S. Hawk air defense missiles and British Lightning fighter-bombers, the U.S. having declined the sale of its F-104 fighter aircraft. Nasser's path to Saudi oil resources was to have been through North Yemen. The lesson has not been forgotten in Riyadh.

The year 1967 hardly weakened Saudi determination to develop credible defenses. As British forces left South Yemen, the National Liberation Front assumed control. They soon began to support the Dhofar rebellion in Oman, to subvert the none-too-stable government in North Yemen, and—with Soviet, Cuban, and for a time Chinese aid—to develop and support radical cells throughout the Gulf. The civil war in North Yemen was still a threat to Saudi security. The kingdom's strategic position was unenviable. With an unstable and Soviet-supplied North Yemen to the southwest and a radical PDRY (formerly Aden Colony and the Western and Eastern Aden Protectorates) to the south, a Saudi policymaker could not ignore the potential threat posed by a possible union of the PDRY and North Yemen. Such a union would then encompass a population greater than Saudi Arabia's, with combat-experienced soldiers and airmen using modern Soviet weapons.

Soviet loss of base facilities in Somalia and their consequent greatly increased use of air and port facilities in Aden for support of the Marxist government in Ethiopia has complicated the Saudi security problem. The June 1978 murders of North Yemen's moderate leader, Ahmed al Khasmi, and the PDRY's relatively pro-Saudi leader, Salem Rubaye Ali, appear to have increased Soviet capabilities on the Arabian peninsula. The assumption of power in the PDRY by Abdul Fattah Ismail, a strongly pro-Soviet Marxist, opens the way for even greater Soviet military use of Aden as well as reversal of the previous trend toward accommodation with Egypt and Saudi Arabia.

The 1967 Arab-Israeli war, while not directly involving Saudi troops, also jarred Saudi Arabia's strategic thinking. First, Israel's occupation of the Sinai brought Israeli military control of the Gulf of Aqaba, thereby exposing Saudi Arabia's undefended Gulf of Aqaba shoreline and permitting Israeli occupation of the two uninhabited but strategic Saudi islands of Tiran and Sinafir in the Straits of Tiran.[24] Second, given the recent close association between the Saudi and Jordanian monarchies and the role of Saudi Arabia as the guardian of Islam's holy places, Israeli occupation of Jordan's West Bank and Israeli annexation of East Jerusalem were events of special political and religious significance for the Saudis. Third, the stunning defeat and humiliation of the 1967 war meant in a broader sense that all Arab countries were drawn more deeply to strengthen Arab defenses. While Saudi Arabia's contributions were obviously to be primarily financial, it is questionable whether the Saudi royal family could have maintained its position within the kingdom had they ignored rebuilding Arab military capabilities. The minimal expectation was a credible force for Saudi Arabia's own defense.

Finally, the 1967 war meant an inevitable strengthening of radical forces in the Arab world, an increased dependence on the Soviet Union for Egypt, Syria, and Iraq, and the rapid infusion of more advanced

weapons into the Arab world against which the obsolescence of Saudi
equipment would become even more stark. As with each Middle East
war, however unevenly, the net strength of Arab purpose had increased.
Saudi Arabia, under virtually any imaginable leadership, could not have
remained with museum relics of military equipment, particularly after
the 1968 announcement of British military departure from the Gulf.
The announcement signaled the end of a comfortable, if at times
humiliating, era in which Riyadh could virtually ignore the defense of its
incomparably oil-rich eastern province and the strategic Gulf waterway.
Oil wells, complex pumping stations, and highly specialized port facilities were guarded by forces trained in obsolete doctrine, and carrying World War II (or earlier) rifles. These troops lacked air support, air
defense, naval capability, or even communications channels into the
waters of the Gulf. The absence of adequate Saudi forces created a
situation in which Iran could dictate policy for the smaller Gulf states,
and where Iran alone would have the capability for intervention there in
the event of extremist political/military meddling. The smaller Gulf
states would then acquire weapons systems to symbolically counter-
balance Iranian and, to a degree, Iraqi power. This, in turn, would have
created a different kind of destabilization for Saudi Arabia in which an
essentially undefended eastern province became vulnerable not only to
larger powers but to possible pressures created by a combination of small
Gulf states or an outbreak of hostilities between Gulf states.

By any standard, and particularly in relation to its major neighbors,
the Saudis worked from a modest base in upgrading their army and air
force, and subsequently their National Guard or White Army. Estimates
vary widely, but in the mid-1960s the army and national guard each
consisted of about 20,000 men, and the small Royal Air Force, only
several thousand.[25] By 1976 the army and national guard are estimated
to have grown to about 33,000 each, the air force to 6,000 and the navy
to 1,000.[26]

In contrast, Iran's army, air force, and navy are thought to number
165,000, 57,000, and 13,000 respectively, and Iraq's 90,000, 10,000, and
2,000 respectively.[27] Based on Saudi Arabia's estimated 830,000 square
mile land area, versus Iran's 636,000 square miles and Iraq's 172,000
square miles, Saudi decisions on force development represented more a
response to regional developments and changes in the Arab world as a
whole than a self-generated desire for military power per se. Saudi
interest in acquiring fighter aircraft beyond the F−5E capability, for

instance, was triggered by the March 22, 1973 attack by PDRY MiG–21s on the Saudi border town of al Wadia.[28]

The Smaller Gulf States

The smaller states of the Gulf confronted the prospect of British military withdrawal with varying capabilities, but in no case was a state totally without a trained nucleus of men generally capable of maintaining internal security and suitable as a base upon which to develop national defense. Kuwait, which maintained a minimal force of some 2,500 at independence in 1961, quickly resolved to expand and modernize this capability following Iraq's threatening moves shortly after independence. Kuwait's eyes were generally focused on the immediate problem with Iraq rather than on a larger regional role of fitting into a systematic defense structure with Saudi Arabia. Kuwait needed trip-wire forces to slow any Iraqi incursion sufficiently to permit the marshaling of an Arab League and/or Iranian counterforce coupled with diplomatic action in the U.N. By 1965 Kuwait expanded its forces to 7,000 men equipped with the beginnings of modern air, naval, and armored capability.[29] As in the case of the rest of the smaller Gulf states, the existence of such a force, however modest, was generally ignored by assessments on the eve of British military withdrawal that emphasized the Gulf's power vacuum on the one hand, and proclivities toward violent upheavals on the other.

Bahrain, originally to have joined the federation of sheikhdoms, formed a small national guard of less than 1,000 men in anticipation of British withdrawal, and Qatar increased the size of its Public Security Force to about 3,000 under the leadership of a former British officer. Qatar's security force originated in the early 1960s following the discovery of oil and was officered by a mix of British and locals. For both Bahrain and Qatar, the primary concerns were internal security and the prestige associated with a new era in the Gulf. The lower Gulf states represented a different situation. The new federation of United Arab Emirates inherited the small but experienced Trucial Oman Scouts as well as the Abu Dhabi Defense Force, which immediately began a rapid process of expansion and equipment upgrading (to include air and naval capability) following British departure. The Trucial Oman Scouts had originated in 1951 under British auspices (initially as the Trucial Oman

Levies) for the purpose of imposing peace among the tribes of the area, whose constant battles made the search for, let alone exploitation of, oil unfeasible. With only about 1,500 men the British-commanded force formed a natural adjunct to the "informal Trucial States Council without any written constitution . . . [which] was established . . . [and] became responsible for the ever growing development programs initially financed by the British government."[30] The Scouts were used by Abu Dhabi and, indirectly, Oman, during the dispute with Saudi Arabia over the Buraimi oases in 1955, in effect taking the oases from Saudi forces in a bloodless expedition. Later, they became active in the Muscat and Oman civil war on the side of Sultan Said ibn Taimur, father of the present ruler of Oman. At the time of British departure, about 40 percent of the force was recruited locally, with the rest consisting of Omani, Indian, and Pakistani recruits.[31]

Increasingly, in the UAE, as elsewhere in the Gulf, a greatly modified leadership and training role passed from British to Jordanian hands. A senior Jordanian general officer now commands the United Arab Emirates forces and is charged with the responsibility of welding the Abu Dhabi Defense Forces and the Scouts, now called the Union Defense Force, into a cohesive, modern, military entity. The mission of the UAE forces, beyond an internal security role, becomes elusive to define. Prestige is certainly a driving factor as an adjunct of the UAE's significant financial resources and power. The UAE forces also reflect the UAE leadership's desire for a charismatic symbol of national unity to help overcome the residue of centrifugal tendencies within the federation.

Oman was, and remains to a degree, a special case in the Gulf. Geographic insularity, caused by the forbidding Empty Quarter desert in Saudi Arabia on one side, and the sea on the other, was compounded historically by the powerfully isolationist tendencies of the prevailing minority Islamic Ibadi sect, which forbade contact with other Muslims. As already noted, British influence has deep roots; in 1921, through an officer seconded from the Indian Army, the British began to develop the Muscat Levy Corps, "composed of Persian mercenaries but later recruited locally and in Makran," which became "a small but well-drilled" force.[32] Acquisition during the same year of "two powerful motor launches signaled a revival of Masqat's determination to control its coastal waters."[33] British intervention saved the sultanate in the war of 1913–1920 with the Imam, the religious and tribal chief of inner Oman who was backed by Saudi tribes, and again during the civil war, which ended in 1959. It was not surprising, therefore, that British withdrawal from the lower Gulf in 1971 left the British presence in Oman unaltered. The British continued to lead Oman's army with some 100 officers (either on loan or under direct contract to the sultan) to operate the small Omani air force with British pilots and technical personnel, including Salalah, Masirah Island, and Beit al Falaj airfields, and to operate the tiny Omani naval force of several patrol craft. Preoccupied with the rebellion of the Dhofar tribesmen, the sultan's forces could not have brought the PDRY-supported insurgency to the successful completion that has since occurred without British and subsequent Iranian and Jordanian assistance.

This evolution in Oman represents the beginnings of an informally operative Gulf security system, without pacts or treaties. Neither Iran nor Saudi Arabia could tolerate the existence of a radical or otherwise hostile regime in Oman because of the strategic significance of the Strait of Hormuz, which forms the narrow entrance to the Gulf. The Saudis, through their acceptance of the Iranian military action, and through various pressures and financial inducements to the PDRY, demonstrated their readiness to cooperate with Iran in matters of common concern. Iran, in turn, after some mistakes commonly committed by forces unaccustomed to counterinsurgency action, demonstrated military skill as well as a diplomatic sensitivity to Arab feelings by conducting a low key campaign entirely within the sultan's effort. Iranian forces were promptly withdrawn from Oman as the rebellion crumbled in 1976.

Another example of the quiet Gulf trend toward military cooperation is the reported plan for Kuwait to utilize airfields in Bahrain, Saudi Arabia, Abu Dhabi, or Qatar for dispersal of some or all of its 36 Sky-hawk A-4M fighter-bomber aircraft in the event of a threat to Kuwait's military airfield.[34] Although a step in the right direction conceptually, such a plan would have been far more practical to implement if Kuwait and her neighbors could have acquired the same aircraft. These could then have been maintained by common ground support equipment, spare parts, and knowledgeable technicians in any one of the cooperating countries. Kuwait's defense, however, required an aircraft with sufficient range and payload to deter Baghdad from freely exerting pressure in the two countries' territorial dispute.

Although impossible to document, an important Gulf development over the last five years has been the trend toward greater consultation and coordination on military and countersubversive matters, between Iran and Saudi Arabia, Saudi Arabia and Kuwait, Kuwait and Bahrain, the UAE and her neighbors. This development, a situation normal between friendly neighboring states, is notable because of its previous rarity. The regularization of these working level, as well as high level, contacts is a natural and essential precursor to the development of any more formal security arrangements.

Jordan: A Special Gulf Role

No discussion of Gulf security would be complete without mention of the special role of Jordan, which though not a Gulf state takes an active part in Gulf security matters. This role represents a little-noticed extra dividend for the long-standing U.S. policy of strengthening the military proficiency of the Jordan Arab Army. Hundreds of Jordanian officers are serving in the smaller Gulf states, often in replacement of British, on a seconded or contract basis. Hundreds of Gulf officers, technicians, and noncoms train in Jordanian military schools. Jordanian personnel have served as advisors to North Yemen as part of the regional effort to reduce Yemeni dependence on Soviet advisory personnel and equipment. These efforts fill a manpower gap as indigenous Gulf personnel are trained and, in the case of the Jordanian general officer heading the UAE's defense forces, provide the kind of experienced, objective leadership capable of melding diverse tribal and other loyalties. Jordan's conservative orientation and continuing close relationship with U.S. military training and doctrine provide Gulf leaders with political reassurance that could not be obtained from any other Arab state with a similar standard of military development. Jordanian intervention capability, as demonstrated in Oman, offers the option of modest-scale support in a Gulf contingency where action by one or more of the larger Gulf states might either be politically unacceptable or need reinforcement. A dispute could occur, for instance, between two smaller Gulf states in which intervention by Iran could generate bitterness that would take years to erase. Jordan, on the other hand, could perform as a neutral acceptable to all with the probable exception of Iraq.

Finally, in analyzing emerging Gulf attitudes toward security requirements and options, the impact of certain common experience merits review. Clearly, the British military could not have been replaced by a system in which European or U.S. military forces bore direct responsibility. The area's experience with the Western-sponsored military alliance in 1955 known as the Baghdad Pact, alone, forestalled even a hint of repetition among nations entering a new threshold of financial and political independence and power. Other than an unlikely collective vote for pacifism, therefore, the Gulf states logically became committed to their own defense. In the pursuit of credible defense forces, attitudes throughout were conditioned by the historical experience of seeing modern (in whatever period) military hardware and the acquired skills to use it employed as a device for foreign intervention and control. Any Western attempts to deny military modernization, therefore, implied a wish to keep the region from achieving genuine independence and national maturity. While financial resources were insufficient, as in Iran during the early post-World War II period, the United States could ration military hardware and assistance on the valid rationale of Iran's national security being better served by economic development aid than by too expensive investment in military hardware. Restiveness and a pent-up Iranian appetite resulted. Nevertheless, the close U.S.-Iranian political relationship was maintained, in part on the compensating rationale of U.S. readiness to intervene in the event of threats against Iran. As both these bases of rationale had become much diminished by the early 1970s, the problem of maintaining a harmonious dialogue on military assistance and sales became far more complex.

CHAPTER SIX

U.S. Interests in the Gulf

Oil and Security: Wartime Transition

Establishing the validity of Gulf defense needs is prerequisite to formation of U.S. security policy. Obviously, however, it does not necessarily
follow that the U.S. should support fulfillment of these requirements.
The inner logic of Gulf defense needs is one thing; the question of an
appropriate U.S. role, another. U.S. policy clearly derives primarily
from our definition of U.S. national interest in the area. In pursuit of
that definition the logical starting point is World War II. As Joseph
Malone notes, "In June 1943, as the combat zones widened in the Pacific
and the armed forces of the United States and her allies expended fuel
at a prodigious, unprecedented rate (as did the industrial plant which
supported them) Arabia took on a new significance to the Western
democracies."[1] Oil, of course, remains the basis of U.S. interest, still
viewed as a critical source of strategic power, but with a sense of urgency
hardly imagined by policy makers initially identifying the significance of
Gulf resources for the West. In a memorandum to Secretary of State
Byrnes dated August 1, 1945, then Secretary of the Navy James
Forrestal wrote, "Because of my firm conviction that within the next
twenty-five years the United States is going to be faced with very sharply
declining oil reserves and because oil and all of its by-products are the
foundation of the ability to fight a modern war, I consider this to be one
of the most important problems of the government."[2] Forrestal publicly
demonstrated his conviction several years later when he withstood
pressure from the Senate Committee on Small Business. The committee
opposed the administration's decision to permit export of 20,000 tons of
steel (urgently needed by small businesses in the U.S.) for the purpose

of building an oil pipeline in Saudi Arabia. Forrestal wisely "took the position that because of the rapid depletion of American oil reserves and an equally rapidly rising curve of consumption we would have to develop resources outside the country."[3]

Iran, which had been a focal point of British-Soviet rivalry throughout the nineteenth and twentieth centuries, was the real magnet for early postwar U.S. strategic attention in the Gulf rather than Saudi Arabia. George Lenczowski observes that, "Iran served as a catalyst [between 1945–1949] which changed the American perception of the nature of Soviet policies in the postwar period, and provided the first stimulus for a radical reorientation of U.S. foreign policy and strategy."[4]

Starting with the relatively limited concerns of supporting British and Soviet wartime occupation forces in Iran and the development of a U.S. lend-lease supply route to Russia from the Gulf across Iran to the Caspian, American policy concepts expanded rapidly. Formation in 1942 of the American Persian Gulf Command, consisting of 30,000 generally noncombatant troops, enabled U.S. port construction on the Gulf, airport building, highway construction, and railway operation, all activities that were to leave an indelible imprint in Iran regarding American capacities.[5] By 1942, Iran asked for American specialists to reorganize its police forces and to advise the finance and army supply division of the Iranian War Department; by 1946, Iran requested credit and military equipment.[6] If the wartime supply route to the Soviets was considered critical, it followed that Iran's security forces had to be trained properly to protect that route from tribal or subversive attack. Numerous other U.S. missions were added, and the U.S. gradually became deeply involved in administrative reform and financial support for the government of Iran. The concept of building a strong and independent postwar Iran as an end in itself became embedded in State Department thinking in a manner John De Novo defines as, "all quite in the Wilsonian tradition with the invocation of the principles of self-determination, anti-imperialism, and free economic competition. . . . [in which] the upshot was the assertion of an American political and strategic stake in Iran."[7]

As European dependence on Middle East oil grew, official American perceptions of the West's strategic stake in this oil expanded accordingly. By 1957, President Eisenhower stated, in responding to his advisor, Dillon Anderson, who had rejected the use of force in retaining access to Middle East oil, "I think you have, in the analysis presented in the letter, proved that should a crisis arise threatening to cut the Western world off from Mid East oil, we would *have* [Eisenhower's italics] to use force."[8]

A Habit Forms: Public Confusion on Energy

This definition, which linked the military security of the West to continued secure access to Gulf petroleum, while remaining a part of U.S. official doctrine, did not penetrate the U.S. national consciousness for several reasons. First, although U.S. petroleum resources were declining and consumption rising, supply and demand fluctuations created recurring doubts in the public mind about the true situation. Second, U.S. government cooperation with the international oil companies in developing and maintaining the import flow of inexpensive oil aroused the opposition of antitrust forces in the U.S. as well as those whose suspicion of oil companies was itself gospel.[9] Third, the importance of the oil equation in the economic and military security of the West increasingly became entwined in the Arab-Israeli dispute. This entwining process grew in direct proportion to Japan's and Europe's conversion from coal to oil after World War II and to the steady increase in U.S. oil imports. For Israeli supporters, therefore, the oil equation frequently was seen as a pressure point arguing for whatever concession Israel was being called upon to make at the moment for the sake of the West's position in the Arab world. The result has been a generally consistent U.S. official definition of national security interest in the Gulf area coexisting with a seriously deficient public understanding of that definition.

Despite widely differing statistical predictions on several aspects of the problem, the basic oil equation remains quite constant in its implications for U.S. security no matter which point of the statistics spectrum one selects as a data base. From a position of petroleum self-sufficiency in 1950, the U.S. by 1970 became a net oil importer and by 1976 was importing about 7.3 million barrels a day (bpd), or 42 percent of its consumption requirements of 17.4 million bpd. By the winter of 1977 oil imports reached 50 percent of consumption.[10]

While in 1973 only 23 percent of U.S. oil imports were from the Persian Gulf, by 1976 this figure had increased to 38 percent and the trend, temporarily disrupted by the advent of Alaskan production, is still rising.[11] Despite the transient current oversupply of world oil, U.S.

dependence on imported, particularly Gulf, oil seems bound to increase. Neither the development of alternative energy sources nor conservation measures appear of more than rhetorical priority in the United States. Despite impressive consumption drops in most European countries since 1973, the U.S. had by 1976 increased consumption 7.5 percent. By the end of 1976 this consumption had jumped another 6 percent.[12] During the first eleven months of 1977, U.S. domestic demand for petroleum soared 6.2 percent over the same period of the preceding year, bringing consumption to 18.2 million bpd.[13] By April 1978, demand had grown to between 19 and 20 million bpd.[14] At that time, U.S. domestic oil production was up and foreign imports down approximately 9 percent from one year before, due primarily to Alaskan oil.[15] However, the temporary surge of Alaskan production represents a fleeting respite. As U.S. demand grows, Gulf production provides the principal potential source.

The Central Intelligence Agency's major study of the problem projects that ". . . world demand for oil will approach productive capacity by the early 1980s and substantially exceed capacity by 1985 [barring] greatly increased energy conservation."[16] The key producing country during the period at least until 1983 is, of course, Saudi Arabia. Even the sobering projection above is predicated on a primarily political Saudi decision to expand production from the current 10 to 11 million bpd to 18 million bpd by 1985.[17] The entire productive capacity of OPEC, excluding Saudi Arabia, is expected to increase between March 1977 and 1985 only from 26.8 to 27.5−29.4 million bpd. Demand, on the other hand, is projected to absorb current and projected excess capacity by 1983 and to create a supply shortfall beginning in that year.

Energy Trends: Impact of the Soviet Equation

The implications of this trend for the strategic significance of Gulf resources are obvious. When the CIA's projections of Soviet supply and demand trends are factored into the political and economic equation, the Gulf's critical importance for the West becomes further magnified. From their current status as net exporters to the West of about 1 million bpd, the communist countries are expected to require at the very least 3.5 million bpd of imported oil by 1985. At worst, declining Soviet production could push this requirement to 4.5 million bpd.[18] Based on current analyses by almost all experts, Saudi Arabian production is the only likely source to even begin to meet vastly expanded world requirements. In the unlikely event the Saudis agreed to double their production (to 19–23 million bpd) by 1985, the effect would be to draw down their reserves so sharply that by the mid-1990s output would begin to decline. Even if current Saudi expansion plans are implemented, the CIA estimates that the projected supply shortfall of as much as 7 million bpd would merely be postponed briefly.[19]

Apart from the political and economic implications of the dramatic price increase for oil implied by the foregoing, an additional pressure is equally, if not more, germane to this study. What would be the effect of substantial Soviet oil imports on their Persian Gulf policy? One far-sighted analyst, Abraham Becker, who addressed this issue in 1971 concluded that ". . . by the end of the decade the Soviet Union and Communist Eastern Europe as a whole will be in the market for Persian Gulf liquid fuel on a relatively large scale."[20] The question he then raised was not of the economic impacts of the likely pressures for catastrophic price rise, but of Soviet behavior in the Gulf. Will a sudden Soviet transition to sharing with the West a dependency on the single area in the world with spare production capacity result in Soviet conservatism that seeks to encourage stability in the Gulf?[21] Or will the Soviets, perhaps well in advance of their import requirements, promote subversive activities aimed at undercutting the West's position in the Gulf, assuring more direct Soviet capability in Gulf political affairs, and developing at least a proxy capability to threaten the West's access to the Gulf production?

Regardless of Soviet political policy toward the Gulf, the very fact of Soviet entry as a buyer in the Gulf market carries with it the potential for creating strains between the U.S., our NATO allies, and Japan as all converge on the same point for the sake of satisfying energy requirements. While the question of Soviet behavior in the early eighties will remain a highly elusive topic, there can be no doubt that the importance of the Gulf to U.S. security interests has increased acutely since 1971 when National Security Council deliberations, made in an atmosphere of relatively relaxed energy projections, already placed a high priority on relations with Gulf states.

All statistical projections about energy consumption and production are subject to wide variation and interpretation, as will be noted in more detail shortly. Virtually no responsible configuration of statistics, however, has yet led to the conclusion that Gulf resources do not bear vitally on U.S. interests, despite the very wide divergence of judgments on what policies the U.S. should follow as a result. Various U.S. actions can effectively raise or lower the equation a bit. Conservation measures, building emergency stocks of oil, and accelerated development of alternative fuel resources will all be influential only to the degree of shortening or lengthening the inevitable span of years (or in a military emergency, weeks) during which the industrial vigor and military capability of the U.S. and its allies will be inexorably linked to the Gulf. Always subject to debate will be the number of weeks or months NATO could conduct major conventional military operations without Gulf oil, or the length of time before severe political upheaval in Japan or Western Europe would result from denial of Gulf oil. But the end result of these debates is the same.

The vulnerability of NATO and Japan to a credible threat itself poses a heavy burden. Some would brush this aside as an anachronism in the nuclear age where the Soviets supposedly would be deterred from threatening or tampering with vital Western interests by virtue of the counterthreat of annihilation. The track of this logic only leads to a world even more painfully balanced on the knife-edge of nuclear terror than at present. Ignoring Western security interests in the Gulf would be tantamount to ignoring the requirement for conventional military forces in Western Europe. The paring down of options to a sole and ultimate response does not appear to promote a more tranquil and stable world. Threats to the West's and Japan's access to Gulf oil could arise under circumstances in which the Soviet role was obscure, highly indirect, or even nonexistent. The West, therefore, and the U.S. in particular, requires the closest kind of relationships with the major Gulf countries, relationships in which the strength of U.S. interest is deeply engaged— politically, economically, and in the security area.

With U.S. Gulf interests based on petroleum it follows that the transport of this resource to the industrialized world becomes integral to any definition of U.S. interest. Just as the critical nature of U.S. interest in a resource area so remote and so vulnerable assumes a strategic significance unprecedented for Americans, some of the geographic factors in the transport equation assume priorities that are practically without precedent. For decades naval strategists, for instance, have focused on the significance of such critical choke points as the Bosporous and the Dardanelles, between the Mediterranean and the Black Seas. Critical as these points remain, it is doubtful if any bear quite the same degree of contemporary strategic significance as the Strait of Hormuz, between the Persian Gulf and the Gulf of Oman, bounded by Iran and Oman. By mid-1977 60 percent of the noncommunist world's internationally waterborne petroleum was passing through the strait daily aboard some 42 tankers.[22] With modern precision-guided missiles, this traffic is vulnerable from shore throughout the Gulf, but particularly so, even with unsophisticated weapons, while navigating the narrow channel along the southern shore at the Musandam peninsula of Oman.

Vulnerable as this passage is to threat or interdiction, however, some reports have exaggerated the problem. The narrowest section of the strait is more than 30 miles wide and the channel along the tip of the Musandam peninsula, while the most direct route, is not the only passage. Virtually the entire area of the strait is navigable, with the depths in the center frequently exceeding 180 feet. Sections of the channel now used include depths below 160 feet. Blockage of the strait by sunken vessels, therefore, would not prove workable.[23] Mines or actual interdiction by warships or aircraft could, of course, be employed to blockade the strait as major acts of war distinguished from the kind of terrorist action sometimes envisioned. But this is scanty solace for noncommunist, as well as Gulf, interests. Increasingly, the Strait of Hormuz becomes a vulnerable aorta between indispensable fuel supplies and the capacities of Western and Japanese industrial and defense organs.

Gulf Power: Soviet Pressures

Finally, of course, U.S. interests relate to the political and economic power of the Gulf countries and, in particular, Saudi Arabia. Difficult, and for some repugnant, as this concept may be, there is no escape from recognition of the Gulf's status as a major world power center. That this may be of a brief duration in historical terms is irrelevant for the purposes of this study. Gulf policymakers will for years retain the ability to call the shots on OPEC prices. Saudi Arabia's leverage, both politically and financially, is unique. With its enormous producing capacity, its potential for expanding production and its relatively modest income requirements, Saudi Arabia is in a pivotal position. Whether one examines such issues as today's oil prices, the industrial world's ability to meet production requirements in the next few years, a Middle East peace settlement, prospects for a continued moderate course for Egypt and Sudan, or the Soviet position in the Horn of Africa and the PDRY, Saudi influence can only be assessed as a major moving force. Iran by virtue of its strategic location, human resources, and military forces also exerts a strong influence, though of a somewhat different order. Iran is integral to the balance of power in South Asia and to the ability of the Gulf countries to provide for their own security. Iran's further particular significance, of course, derives from its presumed continuing intention to remain aloof from oil boycotts applied in the context of the Arab-Israeli dispute.

Soviet actions since British withdrawal east of Suez have consistently added to the degree of urgency surrounding U.S. Gulf interests. The Soviets have relentlessly pursued the acquisition of military facilities in and around the Gulf. India, Iraq, the PDRY, and other Indian Ocean states have so far apparently rebuffed Soviet efforts for permanent base rights. The one instance of Soviet "success" at Berbera, in Somalia, is a case study of foreign policy dominated by narrowly defined military priorities to the point of abject cynicism. In the wake of the 1969 military coup by the Somali armed forces, the Soviets continuously injected large amounts of relatively sophisticated military equipment into the Somali forces. Yet Somalia remains one of the poorest countries in the world, with virtually no internal transportation system and a subsistence economy. Any positive Soviet impact on Somali economic problems remained nil throughout the years when extremely costly Soviet military facilities were being developed at the port of Berbera and elsewhere in Somalia.[24] Throughout, the Somali leadership remained forthright and outspoken regarding its intentions to incorporate, by military force, if necessary, the large portions of Ethiopia and Kenya inhabited by Somali-speaking nomads. The Somalis also served as a principal supporter of the liberation movement in Ethiopia's Eritrea province.

Finally, as the well-equipped Somalis began to undertake at least a part of their irredentist mission, in the Ogaden area of Ethiopia, the Soviets tried to straddle the problem by providing large-scale military assistance to Ethiopia, ultimately including thousands of regular Cuban forces. The resulting Soviet ouster from Somalia in 1977 deepened the Soviet military commitment in Ethiopia where, among other insurrections, the Eritrean liberation struggle seems marked for suppression despite long-standing earlier Soviet material and moral support for the movement. Pity the Soviet ideologue responsible for first rationalizing

Somali irredentism and then Ethiopian territorial integrity, with a brief stint at both tasks simultaneously.

The cynicism and political clumsiness of these actions work to the long-range benefit of U.S. Gulf interests as virtually all the states of the area ponder their own vulnerability to Soviet/Cuban intervention. In another sense, however, the brute military success of Soviet action conveys an element of intimidation into the political calculus of regional politics, not only of the Gulf, but of the wider Indian Ocean and African area.

Soviet political rashness is as arresting as the demonstration of their logistics capability. Since the global Soviet naval and air exercises in 1975, called OKEAN 1975, the Soviets have repeatedly displayed their ability to intervene militarily throughout much of the world. OKEAN brought a particular focus on Gulf oil resources and the associated tanker routes, as has the subsequent intervention in Ethiopia. During OKEAN, Ilyushin II−38s based in Berbera operated with the Soviet navy in the Arabian sea and were further supported by Tupolev 95s which came from Central Asia over Iran.[25] Apparent Soviet determination to regain a military foothold abutting the entrance to the Red Sea, either in Ethiopia, the PDRY, or both, creates natural concerns for Western tanker traffic and ironically, for both Saudi Arabia and Israel, apprehension about growing Soviet influence at a choke point of shared strategic significance.

The policy conundrum arises because, unless Soviet energy problems are considerably more severe than CIA estimates, they do not have vital national security interests at stake—that is, unless an increasing capability to cripple Western military power and industry by easy sea interdiction becomes included among Soviet vital national security interests. Why have the Soviets so overextended themselves politically in an arena of such clear Western priority? Soviet inability to form genuinely close and mutually supportive long-term relationships with states in the region suggests that the current military adventurism may succeed only as a short-lived expedition. The cumulative effects of similar expeditions over time, however, could prove catastrophic in the absence of unmistakable U.S. resolve in fostering its own relationships in the area.

CHAPTER SEVEN

U.S. Policy in the Gulf: Supporting U.S. Interests

Conclusions of the National Security Study Memorandum (NSSM), prepared as a U.S. options paper for the Gulf in anticipation of British withdrawal, appeared blandly in August 1972 as a statement of principles:

- Noninterference in the internal affairs of other nations.
- Encouragement of regional cooperation for peace and progress.
- Supporting friendly countries in their efforts to provide for their own security and development.
- Encouragement for the principles enunciated in the Moscow Summit of avoiding confrontations.
- Encouraging the international exchange of goods, services and technology.[1]

For this study, the key part of the statement by Assistant Secretary of State Joseph Sisco noted, "In the security field, we have for a number of years assisted in the modernization of the armed forces of Iran and Saudi Arabia to enable them to provide effectively for their own security and to foster the security of the region as a whole," and with reference to the smaller Gulf states U.S. intent was to leave the door open for "modest amounts of training and equipment," but to stress the "focus of American technical help . . . on the improvement of the infrastructures of the civilian side of the governments and economies to strengthen the fabric of these rapidly developing societies."[2]

In effect, Iran and Saudi Arabia were to receive increasing U.S.

support for the sake of their own strength and for keeping peace in the region. Clearly, these two nations had to cooperate for the policy to be effective. For the two nations to assume the stature required for their role, the U.S. had to avoid a direct security responsibility. The small naval facility the U.S. had maintained at Bahrain since 1949 would be continued in its essentially diplomatic role in which one lightly combatant flagship and two destroyers on a rotational basis were to continue the demonstration of U.S. interest, as opposed to a combatant intervention capability. The statement reemphasized for the U.S. its strong economic role in the Gulf, in oil, and in U.S. technological contributions.

U.S. Imperial Presence or a Strengthened Gulf

Several salient factors dominated the thinking of practically all of the officials who worked on the Persian Gulf NSSM. First, post-Vietnam American public feelings alone virtually ruled out a direct U.S. military role in which our forces would replace the British. Second, any U.S. assumption of such a role not only would have become an acutely divisive force in the Arab world, but would have been unacceptable to Saudi Arabia's and Iran's growing sense of national stature. Because subversion and political instability were recognized as the principal threats to Gulf security, any option, which by its requirement for land bases or formal pacts provided attractive targets for pro-Soviet or other radical groups, became automatically counterproductive. As noted above, U.S. policy in the Gulf had long encouraged Saudi and Iranian economic development as well as an increasing defense capability. These goals could remain consistent only with a U.S. acceptance of both countries as competent graduates from the defunct protectorate system.

Many observers did not agree, for the most part on the theory (1) that the Gulf's primary jeopardy arose from conventional outside military threats against which Gulf defenses were inadequate, and (2) that Iranian-Saudi antagonism, far from favoring the kind of bipolar cooperation that formed the foundation of U.S. policy, would generate open conflict. One writer predicted in 1970 that British departure would bring the Soviet navy into the Gulf area as a replacement, or precipitate a breakdown of order in which Soviet clients would square off against U.S. clients. Or, he believed, the West would have to replace the British with a new imperial presence involving an Indian Ocean fleet, "built around the core of helicopter carriers designed to land troops and a full complement of military equipment in short order," backed up by reserve units either based in the area or available readily by airlift.[3] The goal was familiar—to "sustain the political stability necessary for the continued exploitation of the area's vitally important oil resources," but the method to achieve that goal was defined as "the imperial one of maintaining a viable order in the Gulf."[4]

An effective Western imperial presence eventually would have required extensive home-porting in the area, and in 1973, for one analyst, "cooperation with South Africa and with Portugal, for the use of Mozambique is essential to security of the sea lanes."[5] The difficulties of finding acceptable host countries for home-porting and basing of U.S. forces obviously involve so strong a mixture of U.S. political and moral sensibilities with post-colonial political sensitivities of the potential host countries as to deter more than a cursory examination of possibilities. Basing in Iran would bear particular strategic implications vis-à-vis the Soviets and for the Arab states of the Gulf and elsewhere as U.S. policy would visibly tilt to Iran. Basing in Saudi Arabia would automatically undermine Saudi influence in the Arab world, and would therefore undermine the U.S. interests supported by that very Saudi influence.

Basing in any of the smaller Gulf states would be unacceptable to the two major powers of the area upon whom any workable U.S. policy would have to depend. Certainly, the establishment of any substantial Western base in the Gulf area would place Iraq under practically irresistable pressure from the Soviets for a similar facility. To date, Iraq has been successful in denying base rights to the Soviets.

U.S. rejection of the imperial option in the Gulf area was made in full recognition of the continuing Soviet effort to seek naval and other military facilities in countries adjacent to the key sea lanes for the Persian Gulf and Red Sea. The only Soviet success to date, despite many erroneous press reports about other Soviet facilities, has been in Somalia, as already noted, where massive investment in port, communications, airfield, and missile handling and storage facilities at Berbera apparently have gone down the drain with the dramatic Somali ouster of the Soviets during November 1977.[6] The Soviets have pressed India, Iraq, the PDRY, and many countries along the East Coast of Africa for military rights and facilities, but thus far they have been successful only in expanding the number of ports at which their navy may call. Soviet naval use of the port of Aden in the PDRY has increased sharply since the Somalis foreclosed Soviet use of Berbera, but the question of permanent Soviet access to Aden is open. As recently as October 1977, the president of the Maldives disclosed that his country had turned down a Soviet offer to lease the former British air force base at Gan Island, ostensibly for the purpose of supporting their fishing fleet.[7]

These Soviet initiatives, coupled with Soviet support for Iraq, and more particularly for the PDRY's backing for the Dhofar rebellion in Oman, reveal Soviet determination to buttress their military capability in the area with permanent land bases. Given current Soviet actions in the Horn of Africa, U.S. policy must continue to recognize the high priority the Soviets place on establishing an imperial presence in the area. But in viewing retrospectively the U.S. option in 1971 for launching a similar effort (emphasis on similar because the Soviets never had even the same *theoretical* option as the U.S. for replacing the British in the Gulf), it is useful to reflect that aspects of this Soviet effort have been of net benefit to Western interests. Although the U.S. presence at the remote Indian Ocean island of Diego Garcia continues to attract more widespread adverse publicity than Soviet activities, it is Soviet activities that have helped mobilize Iran, Saudi Arabia, Egypt, Sudan, and now Somalia against Soviet aspirations. Had the U.S. made the same mistake—of trying to found its position on narrowly defined military strength rather than on strong political relationships—the role of the West in the Gulf today would undoubtedly be far weaker and the Soviet position far stronger.

Military Instruments of Foreign Policy

Few alternative options were seen as feasible from the perspective of the Gulf NSSM preparation during 1971. One option certainly without spokesmen within government would have been for the U.S. to cease all military assistance and sales in the Gulf area in order to help stop the so-called arms race, to reduce U.S. association with authoritarian governments, to reduce the risks of U.S. involvement in the area, and to encourage maximum utilization of human and financial resources for economic development purposes. This option, of course, would have included withdrawal of the U.S. naval presence from Bahrain and from the various Soviet-targeted intelligence facilities with which the U.S. is involved in Iran. Unless one were to postulate a total lack of U.S. interest in the Gulf, such an option was not seen as effective in any respect. Iran and Saudi Arabia had long since made decisions to modernize their military forces with, or, if necessary, without, U.S. equipment and adivisory assistance. A precipitous U.S. decision to withdraw from the modernization effort, far from having the tranquilizing effect supposed, would likely have produced serious political strains with the U.S. combined with rapidly executed agreements with alternative foreign suppliers. The decreased political and strategic interest signaled by this U.S. action in all likelihood would have generated a near panic attitude in the Gulf in which new arms purchases exceeded the planned level. The symbolism of a strong and deeply involved U.S. presence is irreplaceable as a balance to amply-demonstrated Soviet ambitions in the area. Were the defense-related pillar of this U.S. presence to have been removed, an overcompensating series of Gulf country actions might well have ensued.

U.S. security policy in the Gulf, as already noted, derived from a combination of Saudi Arabia's and Iran's strong preference for U.S. military equipment and training to implement defense modernization programs, and a vital U.S. strategic interest in (1) fostering the closest political relationships in the Gulf, (2) balancing growing Western dependence on Gulf oil by creating as many areas of interdependence as feasible, and (3) encouraging the development of capable local defense forces. As expressed by a Defense Department spokesman in 1972, "In normal peacetime diplomacy, military instruments can contribute to a political solution; they cannot, in themselves, be a solution."[8] Of the seven military instruments a state can employ to support its foreign policy—permanently stationed forces, facilities or bases, arms supply, training, advisors and technicians, exercises, and ship visits—U.S. emphasis clearly was to be on arms supply, training, and advisors and technicians.

The U.S. presence on Bahrain, called MIDEASTFOR, consisted only of one homeported flagship (an amphibious transport dock ship converted to an auxiliary flagship, manned by 387 personnel) with a combatant capability of four 3-inch 50-caliber general purpose guns, one C-131 transport flag aircraft, rotational visits by two destroyers from the Atlantic fleet, and a handful of communications and support personnel.[9] The mission of MIDEASTFOR began in 1949 as a show the flag, quasi-diplomatic program of rotational ship visits utilizing British naval support facilities. In 1966 the MIDEASTFOR flagship, then a converted seaplane tender, became regularly homeported at Bahrain. The mission remained the same throughout, except to the extent the importance of MIDEASTFOR's demonstration of U.S. interest increased following British withdrawal. To have withdrawn MIDEAST-FOR would have falsely signaled a diminished U.S. interest. To have expanded its role to include an intervention capability, for instance, would not have been acceptable to the Gulf states and would have falsely signaled a readiness to assume the former British role. The low key role performed by MIDEASTFOR had been demonstrated in the 1967 Arab-Israeli war when U.S. Strike Command, MacDill Air Force Base, Florida, assumed responsibility for the evacuation of Americans from the Gulf. MIDEASTFOR activities continued in the same manner, therefore, until the October 1973 Middle East war when the government of Bahrain gave notice for MIDEASTFOR's departure. Following an apparent reversal of this decision and long negotiations that revealed the ambivalent attitude of the Bahrainis as well as U.S. persistence, the status of MIDEASTFOR was finally clarified on July 1, 1977. The homeporting agreement was terminated, but reportedly the two destroyers and flagship *La Salle* will be permitted to resupply at Bahrain's Jufayir port in the future and 60 U.S. naval personnel will remain at Jufayir to coordinate logistics arrangements.[10]

Apart from the annual air defense or naval CENTO exercises in which the U.S. participates, usually with one or two vessels, military exercises have been conducted with Iran only. These have been infrequent and on a modest scale, such as the special forces exercise in Iran July 1–15, 1971. In the Indian Ocean, the U.S. has conducted antisubmarine warfare and aircraft carrier exercises off and on, with the tempo increasing following the freeing of naval assets after the end of the Vietnam War. Increased policy attention was paid to the Indian Ocean as the avenue to the Persian Gulf after the October 1973 Middle East war and the attendant oil embargo. U.S. P–3 Orion maritime patrol aircraft have made occasional stops at Bandar Abas in Iran and Masirah Island in Oman.

Naval exercises are useful in displaying capability, in their training function, and for political purposes at times constituting nothing more nor less than the gunboat diplomacy wolf clad in humanitarian sheep's clothing. They can be useful and, at the same time, when distances are great, also illuminate the exercising power's logistical handicaps as much as his capability in dealing with crises once on the scene. For U.S. Gulf policy, exercises have been and remain an important, but not central, focus. The same may be said for U.S. naval combatant ship visits in the area, most of which, as far as the Gulf proper is concerned, have been made by the ships of MIDEASTFOR. Though infrequent and relatively low key, these military instruments demonstrate an element of U.S. interest in Gulf security. Though bound by no treaty, U.S. forces are displayed as a balance to the heavy proximity of Soviet power.

Given this peripheral reliance on bases or facilities, military exercises, and ship visits, U.S. policy, in response to the decision to play a strong role in Gulf security matters, has come to rely primarily on arms sales and the training, advisory, and technical support required. Before enlarging on this important and controversial aspect of policy, a balanced perspective requires reminder anew that these military instruments were conceived as tools of broader foreign policy. As U.S. interest in the Gulf grew, our diplomatic representation enlarged proportionally, however slowly, in relation to long evident priorities. The American private sector, always the principal expression of U.S. policy in the Gulf, expanded its activities as new oil revenues became available for building the Gulf states' infrastructures. While defense-related U.S. activities made headlines, this important manifestation of U.S. policy remained, and remains today, subordinated to the commercial role of the U.S. in building the basic economies in the area. As the following comments will indicate, U.S. nondefense-related activities far outweigh defense-related efforts in the Gulf as measured by any reasonable yardstick, whether in dollar volume, numbers of personnel, or relative share of the particular country's economic expenditure.

CHAPTER EIGHT

Debates on U.S. Gulf Policy

Following an initial period of relative public acceptance, U.S. Gulf policy became increasingly controversial as Americans weathered the final shocks of Vietnam, of Watergate, and of the October 1973 Middle East war. Although specificity was not the strong point of many critics, as we shall note, much of their concern was based on misinformation. Arms sales, of course, bore the brunt of criticism. Unfortunately, however, the tone of the debates often placed the recipient countries in an adversary role to U.S. interests. At best the debates simply overlooked the inescapable fact that world balances of power would henceforth be profoundly affected by the Gulf's foreign relationships. Some critics seemed disposed to refute or ignore the validity of the Marshall Plan, Truman Doctrine, and Nixon Doctrine, which accepted that the economic health and security of important and friendly countries were linked in a vital way to the security of the U.S. That the U.S. should, therefore, assist the Gulf countries to gain strength was, for many, an argument as unpersuasive as for the U.S. itself to look after Gulf security. Perhaps because of these underlying elements, most criticism did not attack U.S. policy directly, but pried out the arms sales aspects and then asserted without further justification or elaboration that these were the driving force behind U.S. policy.

Particularly as Gulf policy discussions became politicized within the 1976 presidential debates, many aspects of the arms sales programs loomed as increasingly tempting targets through which to arouse vague political emotions. This is not to refute the inherently difficult and controversial nature of arms sales and military assistance as foreign policy instruments. Unfortunately, these vacuous broader debates often obscured evaluation of the difficult issues required for public under-

standing of policy. But as one observer noted, "To many liberal legis-
lators, arms sales are an unmitigated disaster that must be sharply
curtailed. From their perspective, to sell arms is to be an accomplice in
their use, to be a partner in aggression and killing."[1]

In part, these feelings grew out of the ugly history of arms trade since
the beginning of the nineteenth century in which private companies sold
to their own prospective national enemies or to their allies' enemies as
eagerly as to the forces of their own country. Powerful arms manufac-
turers with agents throughout most governments and in the press are
vividly described in the classic, *Merchants of Death*, written in 1934,
particularly in relation to World War I when many soldiers went to battle
against troops using weapons sold by their own countrymen.[2] That
great financial profits were made from those years of agony, of course,
rightly assures the continued historical force of revulsion against indis-
criminate commercial arms sales, as does the sad fact that the World
War I story was repeated in the thirties. U.S. arms merchants then sold
weapons to Japan and Germany, and German merchants to Holland and
other potential enemies, virtually up to the flashpoint of World War II.

As governments finally took control over major arms sales from private companies during World War II, the pattern of selling arms
changed profoundly. But the old image lingered, only temporarily suppressed during the period of strong national consensus for the Marshall
Plan and the Truman Doctrine when enhancing the economic and
military strength of allies became an accepted U.S. mission. When the
cold war subsided, definitions of friend and foe blurred, centers of
power shifted, and the giving or selling of weapons became increasingly
controversial. Vietnam, of course, accentuated this trend and gave an
odious new connotation to the term adviser that affected the image of all
U.S. military or civilian contractor personnel assigned abroad to facili-
tate the absorption of American weapons systems into foreign forces.

Largely in response to public concerns about foreign military involve-
ments Congress during the Vietnam years increasingly took steps to
reduce the numbers of U.S. military personnel stationed abroad in
Military Assistance Advisory Groups responsible for overseeing U.S.
military assistance. As grant aid began to phase down, however, the
Gulf countries, which had ceased to be grant recipients, tended to
remain immune from Congressional action because of the increasing
role of civilian contractor personnel. This evolution generated inevitable
Congressional frustration. This frustration, in turn, was fed by the

public confusion resulting from the fact that most arms sales (or "deals" as usually identified in the Washington press) were being revealed as sensational leaks, with a stress on absolute dollar amounts of sales distorting the actual military implications of the particular sale.

Out of respect for the security requirements of the foreign government purchaser, most sales were classified. In the informal or formal process of the executive branch informing the appropriate Congressional committees, the sale would invariably leak to the press in the same aura of mystery and wrongdoing that surrounded almost all leaks in the post-Vietnam, post-Watergate atmosphere of distrust between branches of government and between government and the public. Thus, revelation of a "secret arms deal" to Iran, for instance, readily claimed lurid front page treatment. Dollar amounts in tens of millions often obscured the basic realities of inflation and sharply increased complexity of modern weapons systems in which a typical fighter aircraft with supporting systems that might have cost $500,000 only five years before would now, for a comparably modern version cost $5 million. Similarly, a Spruance class destroyer that would have cost $120 million in 1974, by 1976 would require an investment of $338 million.

Equally obscured was the difference, for example, between selling a squadron of fighter aircraft or a naval vessel to Germany and selling them to Saudi Arabia. Germany, with an existing modern military infrastructure, including already trained personnel, could purchase the weapons systems at a fraction of the cost to Saudi Arabia. Saudi Arabia would have to institute long-range specialized pilot and maintenance personnel training programs, including language and foreign study, and sign expensive contracts with the selling company for maintenance over the many years it would take before Saudi personnel could be on their own. The Saudis, in addition, might well have to construct a new airfield, acquire new radar and other complex ground support equipment, and in the case of the naval acquisition, order vessels specially designed for Saudi Arabia's unique needs together with port, communications, and the other facilities that comprise a modern naval force no matter how modest in size.

These distinctions have not been recognized by Congress, the press, or critics in the academic world. Arms sales to the Gulf area have been measured in raw dollar terms against all manner of yardsticks elsewhere, to the ultimate confusion of a critical aspect of U.S. foreign policy related directly to national security. The extent to which this tendency has verged on the absurd is amply demonstrated by Congressional insistence on including the dollar amounts of the construction contracts that the U.S. Army Corps of Engineers oversees on behalf of the Saudi government as arms sales. The Corps manages and oversees, but does not itself undertake construction in Saudi Arabia, as part of a long-standing relationship in which the Saudis place great confidence and which forms an extremely valuable part of the total U.S.-Saudi relationship. Although much of the construction is for military cantonments and other military facilities, some is for purely civilian uses. For purposes of American public understanding, the system records, for instance, the multimillion dollar addition of a pediatrics wing at a Saudi hospital (executed by a Korean construction firm), or the construction of a television station, as U.S. arms sales. The cumulative total of management contracts signed and pending by the Corps totals over $18 billion. These contracts span many years and, unless corrective action is taken, will continue to distort the issue of U.S. foreign arms sales.

Between 1950 and 1976, of approximately $31 billion in foreign military sales for the Near East and South Asia region, 39 percent was for actual weapons and ammunition, 60 percent for spare parts, training, construction, communications, and services. In 1976 this ratio widened further as the figure for weapons and ammunition dropped to 31 percent.[3] During fiscal year 1977, Iran's percentage of total purchases for weapons and ammunition was 36, Saudi Arabia's 35, and Israel's 80.[4]

Several further factors color all debates on Gulf security policy. First, there is the widely held perception that Gulf oil earnings represent a gouging of Western resources and therefore that the partially resultant enhancing of Gulf military capabilities should not be a U.S. mission. This view overlooks, at least for 1977, a Saudi-U.S. balance of trade in the U.S. favor despite oil purchases. Second, not only are U.S. sales there to monarchies, but to underdeveloped monarchies. Defense programs involving advanced weapons systems, therefore, have to many appeared as an unprecedented artificial grafting of modern technology to archaic social and political trunks. Loaded with emotive connotations, this impression has not so much been spelled out precisely by critics as it has indirectly threaded itself into the debates.

Implication can quickly suggest that no matter what threats are present or what resources are available to it, a state's defense posture should be designed by a committee of Western social scientists applying a variety of highly subjective value judgments. Such a committee might decide, for instance, that Iran, because of the absence of a modern industrial base or democratic parliament, should be equipped only with World War I weapons despite neighboring Iraq's plethora of modern weapons systems. The other, and equally absurd, end of the debate spectrum would produce the argument that without exception the Gulf states should be allowed to purchase in any quantity all of the state-of-the-art weapons systems developed for NATO use in combat situations quite different from those likely to be encountered in the Gulf.

The following comments review and analyze in more detail some of the principal criticisms of the U.S. Gulf policy.

QUESTION: *Arms Sales Lead Policy*

Despite repetition by various executive branch spokesmen that the U.S. security role in the Gulf represented a calculated tool of U.S. foreign policy, this earlier concept apparently remains stubbornly embedded. For example, in June 1973 one congressman referred to the "seemingly dominant military focus of our Persian Gulf policy and the relative absence of any priority for diplomacy as a means to prevent a conflict or arms race in this vitally important area," and further complained that "simply to curry favor with these governments by selling arms they want can never be an adequate reason for a policy."[5] Robert Hunter, author of many speeches and articles for public figures (including Senator Edward Kennedy and the late Senator Hubert Humphrey), and Associate Executive Director of the Democratic Platform Committee during 1973, presented similar views that tended to pervade much of the criticism of Gulf policy. When asked by Chairman Lee Hamilton (of the Subcommittee on the Near East and South Asia of the Committee on Foreign Affairs) during hearings in July 1973 to state a guiding principal for U.S. Gulf arms policy, he responded, "We should begin by looking at the area in political and economic terms before looking at it in military terms."[6]

In fact, the prevailing tendency to look first at arms sales and ignore the underlying political and economic rationale better characterized the critics than the policy. Critics of administration policy insisted that, "We can't have a coherent arms sales policy unless we have a coherent Persian Gulf policy."[7] Congressman Pierre Du Pont's special study mission to the Gulf during May 1975 concluded that the U.S. "lacks a cohesive sales policy and that the arms sales policy is a 'non-policy'—an ad hoc response to individual arms requests rather than a well-formulated plan designed to protect U.S. security interests."[8]

In the academic world, the impression of military policy leading Gulf policy predominated even among respected area specialists with first-hand knowledge of Gulf countries. Asked during a July 1973 hearing to define the American presence in Iran (other than oil company employees), one such expert responded that the "largest single presence is the military," whose "number is now up to about 6,000."[9] In fact, although the numbers of defense-related personnel in Iran grew considerably after 1973, by 1975 there were only 1,100 uniformed U.S. military, 2,200 civilians working on Department of Defense-related contracts, and 531 civilians working on projects for which munitions control licenses were required, making a total of 3,831 U.S. citizens in Iran employed under defense-related contracts.[10] Of these, only a fraction of the 1,100 uniformed military could be called advisors in the usual sense of the term, because the bulk worked in support positions. The vast majority of the civilians were technicians in training and maintenance functions. But, most important of all, these 3,831 Americans represented only 23 percent of the total number of 16,700 American citizens in Iran at the time. By 1978, 31,000 Americans resided in Iran of whom 1,200 were uniformed military who, when added to the U.S. civilians employed on defense-related contracts, totaled 30 percent (or 9,300) of the American population in Iran.[11]

Obviously, judged from numbers of in-country personnel, the U.S. presence and U.S. policy were focused predominantly on the nonmilitary missions of economic development, trade, commerce, diplomacy, and cultural/educational affairs. Nonetheless, the myth persists for the Gulf area and has been steadily perpetuated even by prestigious sources. An American Universities Field Staff report in July 1976, *Arms and Advisors: Views from Saudi Arabia and Iran*, contrasting previous U.S. advisory emphasis on aid programs and high level consultants for development programs, stated, "Today, however, the typical American advisor in the Middle East is a military man."[12] Yet, the numbers of defense-related personnel in Saudi Arabia as the authors were preparing their material were 300 U.S. uniformed military (most of whom were unaccompanied by families), and 900 civilians working on Department of Defense-related contracts (accompanied by 2,250 dependents), comprising a total of 3,450 (including dependents), or 21 percent of the 16,000 American citizens in Saudi Arabia.[13] By 1978, 30,000 Americans resided in Saudi Arabia, of whom 200 were uniformed military and 3,000 were employed on defense-related contracts, comprising less than 11 percent of the American population in the kingdom.[14] The seriousness with which the authors of the report addressed their data is not enhanced by their statement that in Saudi Arabia "the British administer the National Guard."[15] In fact, the principal modernization program for the National Guard is administered by a private American firm, the Vinnell Corporation. Under a contract signed in March 1973, initially for $75 million over a six-year period, this project is guided by a small U.S. army unit at Riyadh headed by a brigadier general. With a U.S. corporation providing infantry combat training for guardsmen responsible for the security of Saudi cities and oil installations, the unique program represents one of the more significant U.S. security efforts in the Gulf.

Yet, in weighing the impact of the U.S. presence and policy in Saudi Arabia, how can one ignore the far reaching significance, for instance, of SRI International's central role in Saudi development planning, or of several private U.S. corporations in the massive starting-from-scratch effort to build cities, towns, and industries in the kingdom's eastern province? Bechtel Corporation, for instance, holds a multibillion dollar Saudi government contract to oversee construction of an industrial park at Jubail on the Gulf, and another California company is designing the master plan for a similar park at the Red Sea port of Yanbu. The list of American participation extends into every aspect of Saudi development to the extent that the more burning question for American and Saudi social scientists relates to the magnitude of this effort's social and cultural impact rather than to its dearth and the prominence of U.S. military influence.

Apart from construction itself, American firms have extensive responsibility for design supervision and services in the kingdom: engineering services and construction supervision of a desalination plant at Jubail, a planning and design contract for the Faculty of Medicine and Health Sciences at King Abd al Aziz University, a three-year computer services consulting services contract for the same university, a contract for geotechnical and environmental studies of the site of a new campus in Mecca, preliminary work for a master plan for Abha, capital city of Asir province, design of the world's largest central solar heating system at Tabuk, architectural design of a new campus for the University of

Riyadh, and a five-year contract to provide sanitation services for the city of Riyadh, to name only a few.

The impact of ARAMCO alone, so obvious as to be often overlooked, bears significantly on the kingdom's destiny as well as that of the industrial and military strength of the Western world. ARAMCO's gas-gathering and processing project, the largest petroleum industry project ever undertaken, will serve the industrial complexes at Jubail and Yanbu, utilizing heretofore wasted resources to produce enough gas to fuel half the gas-using homes in the United States.[16] These American contributions cannot realistically be thought of merely as implantations upon the raw deserts and shorelines of the kingdom. Intensive human contact at virtually all levels of technology and education is involved for now and for decades to come. The pattern is the same throughout the smaller Gulf countries and across the Gulf in Iran.

One searches the Congressional, press, and academic debates on U.S. Gulf policy in vain for a balanced assessment of the overall U.S. impact in the Gulf. U.S. diplomacy as a component of U.S. Gulf policy is generally ignored. Although some, like Congressman Hamilton, have bemoaned the absence of a more activist U.S. diplomatic role in settling Gulf disputes, in perspective it appears that the Gulf's very substantial, and in many ways dramatic, progress in achieving cooperation occurred precisely because the U.S. and other Western powers consulted and encouraged rather than intervened directly.

QUESTION: *U.S. Policy Promotes Competition,*
Not Cooperation

Although the early bursts of major economic development in the Gulf have spawned a predictable quantity of partly redundant airports and other projects among the smaller Gulf states, the trend toward cooperation in all areas, though quiet, has been persistent. As observed earlier, cooperation between Iran and the Arab Gulf states has been manifested increasingly. Circumstances absolutely impel the trend, throughout the Gulf.

The waters of the Gulf itself form an essential beginning point. A meeting of experts on economic development planning and marine sciences from the U.N. and Bahrain, Iraq, Iran, Saudi Arabia, Kuwait, the United Arab Emirates, and Oman met in Kuwait during December 1976 to consider the environmental aspects of a rate of industrial development on the shores of the Gulf, which a preparatory U.N. mission to the Gulf described as something that "may be compared with a century of industrial development elsewhere in the world."[17] The group noted the U.N. findings that the rate of investment on the Gulf's western shore amounted to $40 million per kilometer.[18] Broad cooperation has developed in solar energy research, the reclamation of deserts, water conservation, and, of course, in the medical area, on which a Gulf symposium was held in January 1978. Regardless of these trends, however, the earlier stereotypes persist. Defense modernization in the Gulf area for the most part continues to be portrayed as menacing.

Many observers assume as a given that an arms race exists in the Gulf. A few simply have conjured it into being by assertion: "There is an arms race in the Persian Gulf."[19] Nowhere does one see a spelling out of precise supporting evidence as to which nations are racing with each other and which weapons acquisitions are triggering the competitor response. Presumably, out of disappointment at not finding in the Gulf the kind of formal treaties, pacts, and other agreements that characterize certain stages of Western diplomatic intercourse, there has been a strong tendency to overlook the growing Gulf cooperation. Defense buildups have accompanied cooperation because they were in the first place not primarily keyed to topical regional problems or disputes. In some cases, where military cooperation, as opposed to competition, has occurred, as in Oman, it has been dismissed as having, "an air of monarchies seeking merely to protect their own flanks."[20] Such an assessment places the Gulf states in a no-win situation. Cooperation has virtually eliminated an insurgency heavily supported by Soviet, Cuban, and East German efforts in neighboring PDRY and brought greater economic opportunity to the long-suffering Dhofari people. Because the states involved are monarchies, however, their action in protecting their flanks is not considered by some critics a worthy or meaningful manifestation of regional cooperation with salient implications for U.S. national security.

Others have suggested that evidence of military cooperation in the Gulf should not be construed as a likely harbinger of cooperation in other areas, noting that, "experience elsewhere belies this expectation."[21] In many ways, of course, joint military action is the most difficult and sensitive kind of cooperation between states, suggesting that recognition

of mutual interests has reached the stage where other forms of cooperation in the political and economic areas may indeed become facilitated.

Certainly, as in Iran's Dhofar participation, most military commitments are profoundly political in that they tend to break new ground in
political alignments. In that instance, regional as well as Arab world
politics were tested. The Iraqi response, an unpredictable element, was
low key. The broader Arab response, more easily predictable given
Saudi backing, was on balance accepting. Iran, in turn, did not over-
play the exercise in a manner offensive to Arab pride, and, most important of all, withdrew her forces promptly once the military phase
subsided, thereby confounding critics who had said Iran was intervening to establish a permanent military foothold on the Arab side of the
Gulf. Soviet intentions and political capabilities in the area were also
tested in that the PDRY either did not request, or else the Soviets
refused, support for an escalated response. Should another military
threat occur in the area, the changed Gulf political atmosphere, for
which Dhofar represents only a partial cause and only a partial effect,
would make cooperation among the Gulf states more readily available.

Samuel Huntington has written that "an arms race only arises when
two or more powers consciously determine the quantitative or qualitative
aspects of their armaments as a function of the armament of the other
power."[22] Such a competition has not been evident in the Gulf. Iran's
military modernization programs were derived from a broad strategic
perception and are virtually unrelated to the extremely modest acquisitions of Saudi Arabia, the state with which Iran is supposedly competing
in order to control the Gulf. Iraq's military buildup over many years
grew from (1) her role in the Arab-Israeli dispute, (2) her bitter feuds
with Syria over ideology and water, (3) her protracted and bloody pre-
occupation with the Kurdish rebellion within her borders, which only
subsided after agreements with Iran in March 1975, and (4) her many
disagreements with Iran.

Now that Iraq's major disputes with Iran have been settled, at least for
the moment, neither country has shown signs of altering its decision to
maintain modern forces.[23] Both have regional roles in which mutual
fears are subordinate. Although, as noted earlier, Iraq has tended in the
past to maintain a general parity of weapons systems with Iran, this no
longer appears to be the case. The Iran-Iraq relationship is one in which
arms purchases are more effects than causes of tension; and, in fact, one
which, rather than supporting an arms race theory, would more readily

support the supposition that the two countries were able to come to
terms, in part, because they were both sufficiently strong to negotiate.
Neither, moreover, was sufficiently strong to triumph militarily over the
other.

Plans to form a Gulf organization to pool intelligence information
and anti-sabotage measures were announced on May 8, 1978, by the
Arab Press Service, a Beirut-based oil and financial bulletin. Iran, Saudi
Arabia, Kuwait, Bahrain, Qatar, the UAE, Egypt, and Sudan reportedly
will develop an Oil Interpol through which protection could be increased against threats to Gulf installations from groups like the Popular
Front for the Liberation of Palestine.[24] The Front repeatedly has
affirmed its intention to carry its battles into the Gulf in response to Arab
negotiations with Israel.

Only in the wider realm of the Gulf's relationship to the Indian
subcontinent does the kind of potential strategic tension seem to emerge
that might one day evolve into an arms race. As noted earlier, separation
of East Pakistan from Pakistan virtually forced Iran into a strategic
South Asian role as guarantor of Pakistan's security. Should India's and
Pakistan's efforts at accommodation, however glacial in progress, fail,
Iran, as the second major power center of the area, may be drawn into a
process that could involve an arms race with India. To date there are
only small signs of such a development, coupled with the preconditions
based on each state's vision of its own major power role in the larger
Indian Ocean arena.

QUESTION: *The Policy is Unworkable in the*
Volatile and Unstable Gulf

Much of the concern about Gulf stability centers in the supposedly
rigid social and political systems of the Gulf countries. Many observers
have drawn on the extensive and valuable literature of modernization
and militarism in the non-Gulf Middle East states following World
Wars I and II and applied this experience to the Gulf area. Some Middle
East states were thought to have grafted Western political forms too
quickly onto traditional societies, while others remained rigid, with the
result in either case that extremist forces eventually took control. The
Gulf, an area characterized by traditional societies, appears at first
glance to represent the quintessence of vulnerability for this kind of

social science model. Medieval societies ruled by sheikhs or monarchs are applying vast and suddenly available wealth to backward economies and, in some cases, developing modern military forces. This is assumed to lead to wide dissatisfaction over the absence of political parties, to military coups, to conflict between tribal leaders intoxicated with a new sense of power, and to a house-of-cards approach in which the fall of one ruler would trigger the collapse of all.

One academic group meeting in 1972 said of the Gulf that "local stability is fragile [and] . . . at the mercy of Iranian contempt for Arabs, which most Arabs return . . . [and] is also affected by the wind of change blowing in from the radical states of the Arab world and could be at the mercy of a local proliferation of Arab armies."[25] In succinct summation of the impact of oil revenues the report noted, "This sudden wealth falling on a poor area can be likened to rain. Falling in moderation it is beneficial; falling in torrents, it is like a flash flood that sweeps away all familiar landmarks."[26] Huntington views the centralized power required by monarchies as a force that "makes difficult or impossible the expansion of the power of the traditional polity and the assimilation into it of the new groups produced by modernization."[27] As a result, he says, "the future of the existing traditional monarchies is bleak. The key questions concern simply the scope of the violence of their demise and who wields the violence."[28]

Although there is continuing validity to these conventional interpretations, the Gulf states, excepting in many ways Iran, are undergoing an unprecedented transformation. While hardly immune from the tensions arising from rapid economic change within an authoritarian framework, in actuality they do not manifest the seething qualities so many have depicted. First, as already noted, the so-called wind of change blowing to the Gulf from the radical states is generally uncaptivating. Iraq's singular lack of political development and economic success certainly does not engender envy from the other Gulf states, any more than does the PDRY to the south. Both states undoubtedly continue to operate subversive cells in most of the Gulf countries, but from where is their larger support to be developed? Of all the Arab Gulf states only Bahrain has the kind of long-established largely indigenous labor force that constitutes, chiefly by virtue of Bahrain's dwindling oil production, a potential revolutionary force.[29] For the most part, the backbone of the Gulf states' labor force is expatriate. These expatriates, under a variety of temporary permits, come to the Gulf from, among other places,

North Yemen, India, Pakistan, or Arab countries with economies less dynamic than those of the Gulf states.

The situation in Saudi Arabia, for instance, in many ways presents new ground for social science analysts. This uniqueness casts considerable doubt about the applicability of conventional assessments of the impact of modernization. Somewhat over half of the current Saudi labor force consists of Yemenis, Pakistanis, Indians, South Koreans, Filipinos, Turks, and so on. Should present trends continue, by 1980 two-thirds of the labor force may be foreign.[30] The presence of so many foreigners inevitably creates problems within a conservative society, including an increase in crime. Were tensions to mount widely in the kingdom, however, over half the labor force would be likely to remain uninfluential in any consequent agitation. Saudi authorities have been quick to deal with strikes or work stoppages by foreign workers; were labor elements to precipitate a major action against the government, it seems reasonable to assume that the very strong sense of Saudi nationalism would quickly coalesce. Saudi Arabia is not a Gulf exception. Excluding Bahrain, it was estimated in 1972 that "In the oil-producing Gulf city-states . . . foreigners account for not less than 50% of the total population."[31] This percentage presumably has since increased. While such large numbers of foreign workers may occasion severe social and political problems over time, for the moment they appear to generate more stability than unrest. Kuwait, of course, represents a special situation where substantial numbers of well-educated Palestinians occupy important positions in government.

A second major factor casting doubt on many of the conventional prognoses about Gulf stability is the existence of far more division of power in the states than is commonly supposed. This division has not been manifested by typical Western forms, except for the now aborted national assembly experiments in Bahrain and Kuwait. But for each ruling family, division of power has been nonetheless real, allowing again for a unique Iranian situation. Vast development programs and complex linkages to foreign companies and markets have made it impossible for any ruling family to hold all the reins. Rulers have become dependent on their bureaucracies, their experts, and on the ability of many programs to function purposefully together. In addition, many in the Gulf societies, who were only a few years ago in relatively menial positions, have now acquired stature and wealth. The societies are not immobile.

Viewed from a Western standpoint, or from the perspective of a frustrated Gulf intellectual or journalist, these changes may appear insignificant in relation to requirements for democratic expression. Seen from within the affected sectors of the societies themselves, however, and against the backdrop of the last several hundred years of history, the changes represent dynamic motion. Coupled with the fact that education at all levels is available to youth and that the full trappings of the welfare state, best exemplified in Kuwait, abound, many of the predictable pressures have yet to emerge. Inevitably they will, but probably not by way of the radical Arab states so much as from those who have been educated in Western democracies.

Another popular misconception is that of rulers being snuffed out of power by assassination and coup. The misconception requires balancing. The al Khalifa family has ruled Bahrain for nearly 200 years, with each ruler averaging 20 years in power.[32] Qatar has had one-family rule since 1822, Dubai since 1833, and Abu Dhabi has had only twelve rulers since 1793. Some would argue that this pattern represents a stagnation overripe against the powerful currents of modernization. Gulf history since British departure, however, does not suggest that the institution of the Gulf ruler is incapable of adaptation or transition; witness Qatar's change of rule from Sheikh Ahmed to Sheikh Khalifa in February 1972 and the smooth transition of power in Saudi Arabia following the assassination of King Faisal. Tribalism is, of course, still the base of Gulf societies, and its erosion must be sufficiently rapid to accommodate the changes brought by the oil boom and yet gradual enough to keep the societies stable while new concepts of loyalty evolve. To date, most Gulf states are ruled by monarchies reasonably sensitive to the evident dilemmas of this process.

Of all factors most helping stability in the Gulf is the acuteness of the interdependence of the Gulf states themselves, on the one hand, and between the Gulf states and the industrial world, on the other. The wider Arab world shares in this interdependency. In contrast to the days when Nasser coveted Gulf oil, these now greatly increased resources are available within the Arab world in an abundance undreamed of by Nasser. Whether it is the rebuilding of Lebanon, Egypt's financial plight, or the prospect of major resource commitment for an eventual Palestinian national reconstruction, Gulf resources are crucial.

The wider Arab world retains a stake in Gulf stability and productivity as a phenomenon probably for many years inseparable from

Western technology and cooperation in marketing. Within the Gulf, mutual restraints and dependencies are even more obvious. Various rulers could come and go, and if production and transport of oil were unimpeded and unthreatened, the Gulf would presumably adapt.

Quite opposite to the house-of-cards model, however, if one Gulf country were to be captured by radical forces threatening to disrupt the flow of oil, it seems reasonable to postulate a kind of Gulf antibody reaction in which each state would contribute whatever it could against the infecting element. To a degree unprecedented among any group of adjacent countries, the Gulf states' incomes are undiversified, vulnerable, and therefore interdependent. This is not, however, to portray the Gulf as immune from upheavals. Certainly, the Arab-Israeli dispute could eventually radicalize the Arab side of the Gulf. Iran's political background and stage of economic development pose distinct problems. Reasonably, we must assume that changes in the forms of governing in the Gulf countries will occur over time. But it would be as misleading to ignore the strong factors working for stability as it would to focus solely on the negative aspects of the equation, leaving the process of public understanding to articulate only with the stereotypes of volatile, unstable, and explosive.

QUESTION: *Gulf Arms Sales Threaten the Delicate Military Balance in the Middle East*

For many years the term "delicate military balance in the Middle East" has served as a euphemism for "overwhelming Israeli military superiority." The balance never has become delicate. Neither U.S. nor Israeli policymakers were prepared to live with a situation in which intervening U.S. forces might be required to prevent an Israeli defeat. Even less desirable would be a military crisis in which a threatened Israel were provoked to use nuclear weapons. Misunderstanding of the balance issue, however, and doubts about the validity of U.S. intelligence assessments on the subject unfortunately were increased by the October 1973 war. Israel's initial setbacks were often portrayed as an indication of faulty U.S. assessments regarding the margin of Israeli superiority. Opening Arab attacks, it was said, sent the Israelis reeling and, therefore, Israel, in a situation of delicate security, required dramatic new levels of assistance to redress the balance. In fact, once Israeli mobilization occurred, the length of time required to defeat Arab forces coincided precisely with previous U.S. assessments. Although the 1967 war began in entirely different circumstances, U.S assessments about Israel's margin of superiority at that time also proved accurate. For current perspective we need to add the substantial degree of Egyptian post-October 1973 demobilization and the degradation of her air force and ground air defense system due to Soviet denials. Comparatively, Israeli military strength and readiness have increased since the war by a factor of two or three. For these reasons, U.S. officials can speak with some confidence on the balance issue. The political connotations of the balance issue are delicate both in the U.S. and in Israel. The military balance itself is not.

Against this background, therefore, current concerns about the impact of Gulf arms sales on the Arab-Israeli balance can be focused. Iran, as the only Gulf country now with a significant military force and also a major purchaser of U.S. arms, also has a long-standing special relationship with Israel that alone seemingly disqualifies Iran as adding to the military threat against Israel. Even some members of Congress, however, apparently fear that Iranian forces may some day join the Arab states in a war against Israel. These fears were in part generated by the Shah's major diplomatic rapprochement with Egypt in early 1975 during which he pledged investment of over $800 million in Egyptian development projects and called for Israeli withdrawal from the territories occupied in the 1967 war.[33] In particular, misunderstanding arose when the Shah was quoted in the Beirut magazine, *Al Hawadess*, as saying, the next "Arab-Israeli war will be our war."[34] The Iranian Foreign Mininstry and the Shah personally disowned the quote. For Iran, the vast bulk of whose military equipment is of U.S. origin, to join an attack on Israel would mean an immediate cessation of all U.S. technical support and shipments of military spare parts. As Iran will be dependent on this support for many years, an attack on Israel would mean Iran opting to become perhaps 75 percent defenseless in sophisticated weaponry within days. Given Iran's geographic position, such an act does not appear credible.

Of more fundamental importance for Iran would be the very obvious and critical jeopardy created for the full scope of her political relationship with the United States. With this in mind it strains the imagination to devise a scenario in which any gains Iran might postulate from a campaign against Israel could outweigh the disastrous consequences of

(1) immobilizing a defense system developed at a cost of billions, (2) attacking a country, which in a subtle way constitutes for Iran a strategic hedge in circumstances where Arab power might mobilize against Iran, and (3) forfeiting the entire political and economic spectrum of its U.S. relationship through which Soviet power is balanced and on which Iran's economic progress heavily depends. This is not to mention the formidable logistic problems Iran would face in any but a token effort against Israel. Iran's force development is designed for mainland defense plus an Indian Ocean naval and air surveillance capability, not for the large-scale deployment of heavily equipped expeditionary forces over long distances. Finally, it is difficult to imagine an incentive sufficiently powerful for Iran to expose its highly concentrated and vulnerable oil installations to retaliation by Israel's air force.

Assuming the elimination of Iran as a potential opponent of Israel, the furor regarding arms sales to the Gulf focuses primarily on Saudi Arabia. Sales to the Saudis, just like sales to Iran, Israel or any other country are examined prior to State Department approval to determine "how the proposed transfer affects the regional military balance, regional military tensions, or the military buildup plans of another country."[35] Although this process is subject to skewing efforts by parochial industry, U.S. army, navy, air force, or other interests, its normal course winds exhaustively through the careful review of many civilian and military experts. Their final recommendation can, of course, be ignored by the secretary of state or the president, who may also preempt the entire process (as exemplified frequently in past Israeli and Iranian sales) by agreeing to a particular sale in advance of a review process. Given the intense scrutiny of foreign weapons sales by Congress today, however, this kind of bypassing appears increasingly unlikely, even in the case of Israel, the country most frequently affected in the past. Congress itself must now approve all sales over $25 million. Staff members of Congressional committees and individual members of Congress are often briefed thoroughly in advance of any public or closed hearings on the sale. In short, critics can hardly charge today that commitments are made in the absence of study and consultation.

Yet, otherwise responsible and knowledgeable individuals continue to level unsubstantiated broadsides such as, "The United States is providing arms to both Israel and its Arab enemies. Many recent arms sales negotiations appear to be random and ad hoc, often with unforeseen or unintended consequences. These signs indicate a dangerous trend toward a return to the unstable multipolar condition of the pre-World War I and II days with profit-seeking arms companies hustling business much as they did then."[36] This kind of generalized allegation defies close analysis. Does the writer mean that, in providing arms to Jordan, for instance, U.S. policy is responding to corporate pressures? U.S. arms sales or grant military assistance to Arab countries represent the most careful kind of weighing of political interests where, as in the case of Jordan, the policy has been demonstrably successful. Jordan's forces have certainly felt denied many of the more modern weapons available to their potentially hostile neighbors, Syria, Iraq, and Israel. Jordan, however, as Israel has recognized, continues to play an important regional balancing role that requires air and ground forces with modern capability short of that degree which might generate undue temptation to turn on Israel, but sufficient to deter Syria and/or Iraq. To whatever extent there is room for optimism about a peace settlement process in the Middle East, a reasonably strong Jordan is obviously a key element.

What else could the writer mean? The sale of a few C−130 transport aircraft to Egypt or the sale of 36 A−4M Skyhawk fighter aircraft to Kuwait, both of which rested on carefully weighed political/military assessments exhaustively discussed by Congress and the press? Or could the writer refer to Saudi Arabia where all U.S. programs are evaluated on both sides for years prior to presentation to Congress for approval? What may appear as a random and ad hoc negotiation within the news story context far more likely represents the culmination of years of study and discussion. The Saudi request for U.S. assistance in modernizing the National Guard, for instance, occurred in the spring of 1971 and was followed by an initial survey by a U.S. army colonel in August and September 1972. One year later, during July and August 1973, a U.S. army colonel assisted by 21 specialists made a full survey following the signing of a letter of intent by the Saudis in April.

In 1976 an extensive survey of Saudi National Guard logistics requirements was made as well as a technical assessment of the Guard's communications needs. Similarly, the first U.S. study of Saudi naval requirements was undertaken in 1968, but it was not until February of 1972, following further intensive study and discussion, that the final agreement was signed. An overall U.S. defense study of Saudi army, naval, and air force development was requested by Prince Sultan, minister of defense and aviation, in December 1973. A large team of U.S. Joint Staff specialists from the three U.S. services spent April and

May 1974 in Saudi Arabia assessing Saudi needs. Their report was drafted in June and finally released to the Saudis in September. This pattern scarcely reveals an ad hoc approach to defense matters by either government.

Critics of U.S.-Saudi arms sales policy have even gone to the extent of questioning the appropriateness of a modern air defense system for the vast kingdom. The initial letter of intent for this system was signed in December 1965, and, as the surface-to-air defensive missile system became expanded and upgraded to the improved Hawk, additional missiles became a natural sales addition. To Congressman Benjamin Rosenthal, however, the proposed sale in October 1977 of 580 air defense missiles, which would bring the Saudi total to 1200 "would alter the balance of power" in the area.[37] Was the congressman saying that there is a magic point beyond which the air defense of Saudi Arabia is no longer in the interest of the United States? Was he talking about Iranian or Iraqi fears of an excessive Saudi ability to defend its air space? Presumably he was not, but rather was, as with the sales of other items to the Saudis, objecting on the basis that the weapons somehow could be used against Israel. Were either some of the Saudi launchers and/or its missiles moved (in violation of the standard sales clause prohibiting the transfer of weapons to any third country without permission) to Jordan, for instance, the only other Arab country with Hawk missiles in its inventory, what criteria could possibly determine that the entire Arab-Israeli balance would be upset?

Does this mean, for instance, that Jordan is only to be permitted a few missile rounds in its self-defense and that the addition of some Saudi missiles would become destabilizing? Sadly, those who most concern themselves with arms escalation in the Middle East when it comes to Arab sales are the very ones who have historically put most pressure on the overall Middle East arms problem. Political pressure has often been used to bring about U.S. sales to Israel that otherwise would not have been made on the basis of professional military judgments.[38]

When Israel's important and valid needs have already been met, the process of going beyond this to new levels of technology has merely provoked a Soviet response tending to nullify whatever Israeli gain might have occurred. The resultant infusion of higher and higher levels of weapons technology into Egypt, Iraq, and Syria, moreover, has been one of the most powerful forces working on Iran, Jordan, Saudi Arabia, and the other moderate Arab states to acquire more up-to-date weapons in order to maintain the credibility of their defense posture and the morale of their soldiers and airmen.

There is a further complication from efforts to count rifle bullets and combat boots going to the moderate Arab states and to Iran, while at the same time ignoring prudent professional assessments by oversupplying Israel. First, as the reliability of the U.S. as a military supplier, maintainer, and trainer is brought increasingly into question, the tendency of countries relying on U.S. support is to hedge against U.S. restrictions by buying more, stockpiling more, and complicating their already difficult logistics situations by concluding backup sales arrangements with European countries. The action of the critics in this sense works to exacerbate the problems to which their criticism was directed. Second, Israeli security interests are damaged as the moderate Arab states lose a portion of the stature that derives from their strong, visible U.S. link.

The important relationship between U.S. sales to Israel and the problems of military balance throughout the Middle East must be recognized. The assumption, moreover, that every weapons sale to an Arab country, or to Iran, represents a weakening of Israel's security posture must be discarded. A diminishing U.S. role in the Gulf area's defense modernization process would unquestionably bring increased sales by the French and others in a process that would erode those elements of control now possessed by the U.S. In such a process, moreover, the French advanced Mirage F1 would become part of the Saudi inventory and therefore available to other Arab countries with F1 inventories. In effect, therefore, by blocking a U.S.-Saudi sale of the F−15 Eagle, an aircraft not in the inventories of other Arab states and, therefore, not readily transferable, Congress would have assured wider proliferation of the more easily interchangeable F1. The F1 would also become available to the Saudis three to five years in advance of the F−15.

A full understanding of the consequences of a sharply expanded French role in Middle East arms sales requires appreciation of the differences between French and American sales motivations. For the U.S., such sales are merely helpful for balance of payments purposes and in lowering unit costs of weapons systems for its own armed services. For the French, however, a foreign sale may make the difference between the financial ability to produce the system in the first place, or the requirement alternatively to purchase a foreign system. For France, therefore, various restraints that might reduce the numbers of weapons for a given sale, or might deny the sale in the first place, must be weighed against the prospect of continuing French ability to retain an independent defense industry. This choice brings into play the very basis of French foreign policy, national independence, and world role. Given the opportunity, therefore, French weapons are likely to be proliferated at a sharply increased rate, in the absence of American competition.

The problem of conveying the sense of purpose upon which U.S. arms sales hopefully will continue to be based arises from the trend already identified, from bipolar to multipolar foreign policy. The bipolarity that once made for simple decisions on security assistance has now become a stale and risk-laden formula for world order. Simply because the U.S. is confronted with a more complex global political system in which the growth of new power centers requires a more sophisticated diplomacy and consequently a more diffuse security policy, surely is no reason to long for a return of the cold war. The simplistic accusation that the U.S. is arming both sides in the Arab-Israeli conflict implies that the U.S. either has no important interests in the Arab world or that these interests are such that the U.S. could have developed the same level of relationship with the key Gulf countries without a strong military assistance and sales policy component.

Genuine fears for Israeli security, as opposed to exploitation of the Arab military sales for various political purposes, arise because of a misunderstanding of (1) the technical problems involved in transporting and maintaining weapons systems from country to country or from one army or air force to another, and (2) the nature and degree of Israeli military superiority over opposing forces. While both questions are major topics in themselves, they require brief further comment. First, modern weapons systems, unlike the rifles and cannons of old, cannot be passed from army to army or air force to air force in boxes and then speedily assembled for combat. The backup ground systems to service a modern fighter aircraft and its weapons, for instance, are enormously complex, bulky, and critically dependent not only on a constant pipeline of spares from the manufacturing country, but in many cases upon the full-time ministrations of foreign technicians. The same is true of the Hawk surface-to-air defense missile system. No Arab country, therefore, could suddenly assign a squadron of its U.S. aircraft to operate from another Arab country not already actively utilizing the same kind of aircraft without months of highly visible preparation and the ultimate cooperation of technicians working for U.S. corporations.

Second, Israeli military superiority, increased markedly since 1973, has never rested on numbers of weapons. Arab forces have always numerically outgunned and outmanned Israeli forces by a very wide margin. Fine as U.S. weapons are, the October 1973 Middle East war showed that they by no means in aggregate represent a technological monopoly. Opposing arguments to carefully calculated U.S. sales to Arab countries, in fact, have validity only in two areas. The first area is psychological. U.S. weapons have a quality of mystique bordering on magic in the Middle East because of Israel's many victories and the consequent tendency of Arab countries to attribute these victories to U.S. weapons superiority rather than to more painful assessments. For even small quantities of this magic to be shared with opposing armies, therefore, can be seen by Israel as a factor bolstering Arab confidence. Second, Israel's objection is fundamentally political. Ultimately, Israeli security rests heavily on American public opinion. Retaining the un-questioned backing of this public opinion was a far easier task in the polarized days of Nasserism and growing Soviet entrenchment. An important U.S. military sales and assistance program in Saudi Arabia, for instance, can be seen by some Israelis and their more assiduous U.S. backers as the intrusion of a threatening political symbolism, which, although militarily inconsequential, must be opposed on military grounds, however specious.

Finally, an Israeli military argument with some validity asserts that each weapons system has its highly individual characteristics and in-evitable vulnerabilities that become evident to a user much faster than they do to opposing forces. A pilot, for instance, who has flown a particular aircraft should have an edge when he subsequently flies in combat against the same kind of aircraft. Much more superficially, the same argument can be made with respect to the Hawk system. There will always be differences of opinion even among U.S. military experts about the bearing of this factor on the military equation. Without question, therefore, the issue must continue to be weighed in all analyses. The problem is manageable in large part because of the highly diverse and complex adaptations and add-ons that form the composite of a modern weapons system. What is made available to one buyer need not be sold to the next. Ultimately, it is by this means that U.S. forces help protect their own edge of superiority; i.e., by withholding from foreign buyers certain critical components essential to unique performance capability.

QUESTION: *Arms Should Not Be Sold to Countries
Unable to Absorb Them*

This argument is central to weighing the effectiveness of U.S. Gulf
policy. Oddly, the absorbability issue is used both to support and to
attack U.S. sales. On the one hand, some observers believe, for instance,
that no country "is particularly bothered by Saudi Arabia's acquisition of
arms, because everybody knows they are not going to be able to use them
effectively."[39] On the other hand, the Senate Foreign Relations Committee on October 18, 1977, adopted a unanimous resolution urging
President Carter to limit arms sales to the Gulf countries out of concern
for the "military balance in the Persian Gulf region [and] the ability of
the countries there to absorb advanced United States military technology."[40] Apparently, what is solace to some becomes a source of
concern to others. There is room for wonder whether the Senate
Foreign Relations Committee would be reassured if the Gulf countries
displayed instant ability to absorb advanced military technology independent of foreign training and technical support. Were this the case,
the effects on whatever military balance the senators were concerned
with would be far more direct and pronounced. Valid grounds for
concern indeed exist regarding any country's absorptive capacity, but in
the sense conveyed by the Senate resolution one is told to worry both
because the Gulf countries are not getting strong enough on U.S.
military assistance and sales, and also because they are getting so strong
as to induce a regional arms race and "upset the military balance."

The compelling need for a meaningful ratio between sales and
absorption relates to basic purposes of U.S. policy, namely, to bolster
and enhance the U.S. political relationship with the purchasing country,
deny the area to penetration by Eastern Bloc countries, and create
strength in the buying country. Should programs falter dramatically or
gross ineptitude become displayed in a combat debacle, blame would be
placed squarely on the U.S. Most major U.S. weapons systems, sold only
on a government-to-government basis, are sought by foreign buyers in
part because of the attendant Defense Department commitment to
continue logistics support for the weapons over their serviceable life.
Adequate training and support therefore constitute a large part of the
U.S. reputation as a reliable supplier. In a sense, the credibility of the
U.S. defense establishment goes on the line with every major sale and
the contractor company as well as the U.S. army, navy, or air force

component involved become participants in what by then becomes a U.S. foreign policy objective—to make the program work. If it does not, adverse political repercussions are inevitable. In policy assessment, however, no definition is more difficult to establish than the criteria for adequate absorption. The dialogue between Congress and the Executive Branch, not to mention between the State and Defense Departments and the purchasing country, is frequently eviscerated of utility as a result.

U.S. concern and frustration arise when trainable manpower shortages in the receiving country cause training schedules to slip and hardware deliveries to exceed the availability of people who can operate, let alone service and maintain the equipment. Often, the recipient country will begin robbing Peter to pay Paul as it draws trained or partially trained personnel away from one program commitment in order to meet schedules for another. The specter of unused equipment deteriorating in storage that so concerns U.S. officialdom, however, may not be apparent to the purchasing country whose sense of urgency may function at a very different level. Once a goal is set, either for a Gulf industrial project, urban development, or military program, the quantum jump forward is perceived locally as being so momentous that slippage of schedule becomes relatively acceptable. Manpower planning in the Gulf until very recently has been either nonexistent in early stages of development, or, in the case of Iran, a sensitive subject on which U.S. pressure was interpreted as a means of slowing military development rather than making that development more orderly in relation to the other requirements of the economy.

U.S. concerns over the availability of trained or trainable manpower, in addition, are often taken to imply doubt about the innate abilities of the indigenous population. In fact, much of the press and other commentary on the problem feeds this implication by unelaborated reference to the country's inability to absorb or operate the equipment. The problem, however, is one of time and adequate training; in no case has a lack of innate ability been identified as an impediment to the absorption of military technology. Iran's F−4 Phantom fighter aircraft program, for instance, which was agreed upon in 1966, had its initial detractors among U.S. officials who felt that Iran could not foreseeably achieve self-sufficiency in operating and maintaining the aircraft. Such predictions proved to be incorrect when by the mid-1970s the Iranian Air Force became virtually self-sufficient in its F−4 program. However, self-sufficiency does not imply freedom from an intimate continuing dependence on U.S. logistics support. Iran's present F—14 Tomcat program although plagued by many problems, some of which are attributable to kinks inevitable in any new aircraft, should eventually reach a similar degree of self-sufficiency. The question is how long will this take and how will the many new Iranian programs like Bell helicopters, Spruance class destroyers, Tang class submarines, AWACS, F—16s, and so forth, with their extremely high technical demands, compound the difficulties in existing programs.

On the more deliberately planned and modest basis of Saudi Arabia's military expansion efforts, some reports allege major delays in availability of personnel for training programs, a situation with "insufficient people in the pipeline."[41] Insufficient indigenous personnel, of course, means increasing the numbers and span of service of foreign personnel to fill the gap. This, in turn, with American technicians, can exacerbate fears of a hostage or involvement situation as will be elaborated below. With the presence of foreign (non-American) technicians, fears of security breaches may be raised where sensitive technology is involved.

The U.S. should not be expected to sell an advanced weapons system to XYZ country, for example, only to find it being operated and maintained for years by large numbers of personnel from countries to which we would not have sold the system in the first place. For U.S. programs to work Saudi Arabia, for instance, cannot simply say to the U.S., "Manpower is our business. Sell us the F—15 and we will find the manpower for training." Nor can the U.S. merely say to Saudi Arabia, "You are not meeting quotas for existing programs, and therefore we cannot take your order for more aircraft even though they would not be delivered for many years."

Older aircraft may actually require more in-country personnel for maintenance than advanced models, whose high technology components in many cases are not repaired in-country in the first place. All modernization involves lags in the development of skills, and, while U.S. programs—military or nonmilitary—must depend on reasonably orderly manpower planning, in no case will U.S. interests be served either by suggesting that the country must remain backward because it is backward or by foolishly agreeing to programs that are clearly doomed to founder.

For the requisite degree of underlying Congressional and public understanding of U.S. military sales to the Gulf area, the purchasing countries will have to subject themselves to an extremely painful open dialogue on manpower availability, an issue militarily as well as nationalistically sensitive. On the U.S. side, in order to achieve this understanding, issues must be addressed for what they are and questions based on absorptive capabilities should not be used as a smokescreen for other objections.

For leaders in either the selling or buying country to ignore these realities displays a cynicism that will eventually create political damage that at home or abroad (or both) will jeopardize U.S. national security interests. Impressionistic assertions, such as Emile Nakhleh's that "in terms of volume and quality, the arms sold to Saudi Arabia by the United States since early 1974 do not appear to reflect thorough planning and direction by the National Security Council," are all the more damaging when made by serious observers.[42] In subsequent discussion Nakhleh merely cites Saudi 1974−75 defense expenditures of more than $1.8 billion as evidence they are arming themselves to the teeth with no explanation of the breakdown of costs as between construction and weapons, the span of years over which payments will be made, the actual military capability to be achieved, or when deliveries of weapons will occur. Ignored are the years of careful planning identified earlier. Much of the more recent controversy over the F−15 sale to the Saudis similarly overlooked publicly available planning data. Saudi manpower requirements for the 60 F−15s were exactingly projected at 900 technicians and 75 pilots based on introduction of the system in 1982. Technicians currently employed on the F−5E and Lightning programs number 1,385; 500 will be produced by the Saudi technical school by 1981 and another 1,000 will have graduated from a special U.S. program. A total of 2,885 will be available, therefore, against a requirement for 2,550.[43]

For Iran, where far more numerous and ambitious military programs are underway, some U.S. involvement came as the result of a decision by the most senior people in the National Security Council that the kind of joint planning acceptable to Saudi Arabia, for instance, was not politically acceptable to Iran where military planning is done principally by the Shah. While several Iranian military programs have evidenced serious indigestion problems, the U.S.-Iranian political relationship has yet to suffer as a result. What may appear as an outrageously lagging and inept program to a reporter who listens to the many tales of woe spun by American technicians struggling in frustrating and not always comfortable circumstances, may be viewed from quite another evalua-

86 THE CLOUDED LENS

tive perspective by the Shah and his senior advisors. The job of the
American embassy and military mission in Iran is to make sure that the
cumulative manpower and other demands of U.S. military programs do
not mount to the point where they will undermine rather than support
our political relationship with Iran. Of the many criteria for weighing
the desirability of a given arms sale, the absorbability factor may be the
most difficult to define, yet most important for the U.S.

Few surprises are welcome ones in diplomacy. The recipient country
as well as the U.S. Congress and the public all need to know as accurately
as possible the length of time U.S. technicians are likely to be engaged
abroad as a particular system is absorbed by a buyer. Also needed is a
clear definition of their involvement, and the similar involvement of any
third-country support personnel who may be required. This definition
would need to include any training duties through which they actually
operate the system, particularly with aircraft or naval vessels. Gulf
countries will have to surrender a portion of what they have regarded as
secret information in return for that greater degree of U.S. public
understanding upon which a more solid military assistance relationship
with the U.S. would rest. Congressional watchdogs and others in the
U.S., in turn, will have to recognize that absorbability projections will
frequently contain variables bordering on the unknown. Who is to say
with assurance, for instance, how long it will take a village youth from the
Gulf area with x years of education to learn English and then become
proficient in some aspect of advanced aircraft maintenance? That many
projections will fall wide of the mark is all the more reason for a
continuing focus on their importance.

QUESTION: *American Military Advisors Become
Hostages and Risk U.S. Military
Involvement*

Initial clarification requires, once again, an appreciation of the actual
percentage of Americans in the Gulf involved in defense-related programs. As we have noted, once facts are distinguished from hasty
impressions, Americans working on projects unrelated to defense out-
number defense-involved personnel by at least three to one. In assessing
the risk of having so many hostages in the Gulf, therefore, it is necessary
to encompass total U.S. policy, not merely U.S. security policy, or the

lack of it, as some would prefer to say. Second, the term advisor implies a far different function from that most of the defense-related civilian employees actually perform. In Iran, for instance, the U.S. military mission of uniformed service personnel numbers approximately 1,200 individuals, of whom perhaps one-third are likely to be administrative or support personnel in no way directly involved with Iranian military affairs. These numbers fluctuate as visiting teams of military experts advising on a particular problem come and go. The large numbers of so-called American advisors are mechanics and technicians engaged in training counterparts.

One major source of confusion on the numbers of defense-related personnel in the Gulf arises continually over the failure to distinguish between employees and their dependents. To illustrate, in August 1975 there were 3,357 American civilians in Saudi Arabia connected with U.S. companies engaged in defense-related projects. Of this total, however, only 1,416 were employees and 1,941 their dependents.[44] Unless one is focusing purely on the hostage factor provided by numbers alone, the distinction represents far more than a quibble in determining the scope of U.S. defense-related effort, particularly when the distortion of including nondefense-related American employees and their dependents is allowed to further compound the problem. The general lack of precision on the subject by many U.S. officials and U.S. media, coupled with deliberate scare tactics on the part of those who are purposefully generating impediments to growing cooperation between Gulf countries and the U.S., provides an unfortunate model. Groups like the Iranian Students' Association offer straight-faced publicity about 100,000 American military advisors in Iran today. The distortion is hardly noticed amid the jumble of disparate definitions and broad exaggerations on the subject. How is a fair public assessment to be made when, for instance, so prestigious a source as the *Christian Science Monitor* on March 8, 1977 asserts that "the U.S. military effort brings over 30,000 American civilian and military personnel" to Iran. The true figure of 9,300 uniformed military and defense-related civilians in Iran by January 1978 has already been noted.

Recognition of these distortions, however, in no way detracts from the need to view the implications of a large American presence seriously. For an area as remote and dependent on air transportation as the Gulf, the practical problems involved in any emergency evacuation of U.S. personnel such as was required for Lebanon are formidable. Critics need to appreciate, however, that the numbers of Americans would be large irrespective of defense-related programs. Similarly, valid concerns over the creation of anti-Americanism apply whether the large presence is military related or civilian. Widespread host country frustration or resentment against the American presence is one thing, however, and terrorist targeting of individuals another. The former has not yet become evident in the Gulf area, while the latter has surfaced in Iran on several occasions, first in a June 1973 murder of an American officer in Teheran, an assassination that one observer has called "indicative of the type of problem to which a higher level of involvement can lead."[45]

This and subsequent tragic incidents involving both U.S. military personnel and defense-related civilians in Iran stem from the careful targeting by terrorist groups whose desire to publicize their cause presumably would have been no less in the absence of the particular Americans selected. That high officials in the American embassy were not selected may either indicate that they had better protection, or, the more likely explanation, that terrorist motivation represented not so much a wide Iranian discontent with the American presence as an Iraqi, Soviet, and Iranian Marxist desire to disrupt America's role in Iran's defense modernization program. If this hypothesis is correct, then the political target for the terrorists was not so much the Iranian people or the Shah, but a U.S. Congress and media already prone to relate events of this kind to our Vietnam experience. During the cold war years, Soviet broadcasts to Iran and radical Iranian criticism focused on U.S. Point Four personnel and activities whose considerable ultimate success was correctly perceived as a threat to Marxist aspirations. As Point Four passed, the profile of Iranian-American military cooperation rose in its place and became as natural a target.

Arguments against the presence of American defense-related personnel in numbers responsive to U.S. security policy needs in the Gulf become most pertinent when touching on the dilemmas presented for the host country and American alike in the event of major conflict. Under these circumstances the issue of the involvement of American personnel would become stark reality. Policy planners on both sides, who necessarily must occupy themselves with agonizing scenarios of this kind, undoubtedly achieve tranquillity only in the continuing major congruity of security policy between the U.S. and the Gulf countries concerned. The specter of an Iranian-Saudi conflict in which the U.S. must choose sides is frequently cited to illustrate the risks of an activist

U.S. security assistance role in the Gulf. We have already noted the unlikelihood of such a conflict, but should it occur U.S. foreign policy dilemmas would not be all that different in the absence of defense-related programs. Diplomatic and military support would be immediately expected by both countries. Were vital U.S. interests threatened by a Gulf war of this sort, the U.S. response would likely be determined by factors far more fundamental than those having to do merely with defense-related programs.

These programs, in fact, serve as a powerful deterrent to such a conflict. They make it quite unlikely that either Saudi Arabia or Iran would embark on a military venture plainly contrary to U.S. interests and in violation of the agreements under which the programs were approved. As noted earlier, modern weapons systems require follow-on logistical support from the selling nation during their functional life-time. The "black boxes," which can only be repaired or replaced with the cooperation of the selling nation, are critical to the utility of the system. Many of these spare parts and munitions cannot readily be stored in large quantities. Furthermore, of course, during the years when the system is being absorbed into the military force of the buyer, the training and maintenance function performed by the seller's technicians and other experts, either in the U.S. or in the Gulf area, is both continuous and essential for sustained usefulness.

Some analysts have missed an important distinction in this equation, however. The buyer's dependency for the most part does not mean an inability to operate the weapons for relatively short periods or that the weapons are "operationally controlled by (private or public) American advisors," or "manned by American advisors."[46] Saudi F—5E pilots, in other words, could today fly combat missions in defense of their air space without U.S. military or civilian contractor involvement other than in the complex backup support systems. The distinction is important in that the Saudis could engage in short-term actions without U.S. cooperation, but not an extended campaign, particularly if it involved operating the aircraft from another country's bases. In the final analysis, therefore, the Saudis, in a situation of urgent priority, could function briefly in opposition to U.S. interest. Neither Saudi mechanical dependence on the U.S. nor the larger weight of leverage provided by the full dimensions of the Saudi-U.S. political and economic relationship constitute a guarantee against misuse.

It could be argued that U.S. dependence on Gulf oil has become so

acute as to virtually forestall application of U.S. pressure, for instance, in
the event of an undesirable (from the U.S. standpoint) Iranian involvement in a Pakistani attack on Indian forces in Kashmir. The resultant
U.S. problem would be diplomatic rather than one in which the presence
of U.S. advisors and technicians in Iran increased the likelihood of direct
U.S. military involvement in Iran's misadventures. Although leverage is
a highly debatable factor, it would be difficult to argue that the absence
of varying degrees of Iranian dependence on U.S. personnel and
hardware would provide the U.S. with an increased opportunity to deter
Iran.

On the other hand, an Iraqi attack against either Saudi Arabia or Iran
would constitute an entirely different situation in which, as one analyst
notes, "American advisors might find themselves participating in . . .
conflict."[47] While the participation would be indirect, American credibility would be on the line and the withdrawal of American citizens in
key support positions could precipitate a collapse of the underlying
political relationships between the U.S. and the Gulf. Such a situation
would involve grey areas of authority and policy where private American citizens would be subject to U.S. embassy advice about evacuation of
dependents and, ultimately, heads of families, but, in fact, responsible to
the wishes of their employers and the dictates of their consciences. In
any event, if the preceding definition of U.S. interests in the Gulf is
accepted, some U.S. action on behalf of the country attacked would
appear mandatory. Presumably, therefore, this action would bear far
less risk if the U.S. role could be limited to technical support and supply
rather than landing marines. From this perspective, a strong U.S.
security interest predating this kind of crisis represents more a factor
working for limited U.S. involvement than for engaging the U.S. in an
immediate direct use of its armed forces.

QUESTION: *The U.S. Should Prepare to Seize Gulf Oil,*
Not Develop the Strength of Gulf Forces

The interventionist approach to U.S. security policy in the Gulf and
toward OPEC falls for the most part outside the realm of serious
analysis. Rather, examination of the arguments of its fortunately few
proponents takes one into a Grand Guignol of exaggerations, distortions, and imperial nostalgia. The policy message of this theater comes

full circle back to Portuguese and subsequent European destruction and seizure in the Gulf for economic control.

The confrontationists, however, have added their bit to public confusion about Gulf policy and for that reason require comment. Robert Tucker's articles of January 1975 and 1977, Edward Friedland's, Paul Seabury's, and Aaron Wildavsky's, *The Great Detente Disaster: Oil and the Decline of American Foreign Policy*, published in 1975, and the "Miles Ignotus" March 1975 article, "Seizing Arab Oil," amply exemplify the confrontational approach.[48] The article by Ignotus, "the pseudonym of a Washington-based professor and defense consultant with intimate links to high level U.S. policymakers" (according to *Harpers Magazine*), was apparently designed to add credence to Henry Kissinger's and James Schlesinger's brandishing of the U.S. military option against strangulation of the West by OPEC. Ignotus, whose faculties of judgment were apparently exhausted by his initial decision to remain anonymous, reduced the OPEC-West equation to Western "appeasement" reminiscent of the day when "men persisted in seeing moderation in Hitler's policies when there was none."[49]

To Ignotus, all in OPEC are extortionists, and the Arabs therein are blackmailers whose excessive demands on Israel will inevitably precipitate another war followed by an oil embargo or supply cut. "Then we go in," says Ignotus, with two U.S. marine divisions, the 82nd Airborne Division plus another army division, for a total of 40,000 men on the ground supported by marine air wings, and "at least four aircraft carriers, 20 frigates and destroyers, and 10 nuclear submarines."[50] Saudi oil fields are the principal targets, and the key staging point for the operation is Hatserim airport in Israel. Morally, the seizure, which could last up to ten years would be justified because OPEC revenues had been used "only to finance the executive jets of the sheikhs and the fighter bombers of the dictators," and because "a somewhat impoverished America [became] surrounded by a world turned into a slum."[51] Starting from this premise that the oil must be seized, therefore, all American security assistance to the Gulf states, including the 1965 sale of Hawk batteries to Saudi Arabia, represent "systems shortsightedly supplied."[52] Ignotus coyly suggests that Iran might be an exception if that country could be persuaded as part of the operation to protect Kuwait from Iraq, grab its oil, and use Kuwaiti production to offset the loss of revenue that would result from lower oil prices.

Tucker, in a similar vein, asserts that only the evident lack of Western will to use force permitted the oil crisis to happen, and defines the simultaneous pursuit of independence for the Gulf countries and interdependence with the U.S. as an "inconsistent response."[53] Because Saudi officials acknowledge that a principal purpose of their arms is to protect their oil, "only the obtuse will ask against whom."[54] Like Ignotus, Tucker targets the shallow 400-mile-long coastal strip from Kuwait to Qatar, which contains "40% of OPEC production, 40% of world reserves and 50% of OPEC reserves," but virtually no trees and no population, in contrast to Vietnam.[55] For Tucker, the "refusal even to consider serious forms of confrontation" in response to the OPEC challenge is "likely to rank among the great blunders of recent history."[56] Loss of American power in the Middle East and elsewhere as a result of the oil crisis, says Tucker, combines with a growing Arab leverage that inevitably means that it is "the Israelis alone who will be pressured into making the substantive concessions needed to keep the oil flowing at a tolerable price."[57]

Friedland and his coauthors share many of Ignotus' and Tucker's assumptions and recommendations, starting with the stark oversimplification that "oil is energy; energy is money; money is control; control is power. Oil in the wrong hands is money misspent and control corrupted; control corrupted is power abused; power abused is force misused. With oil out of control, force follows. With force out of control, so may be the world."[58] Friedland concludes that the West "faces the prospect of choosing between bankruptcy and force."[59] In the process, the U.S. will find that its efforts toward an evenhanded policy in the Middle East represent an "illusion [that] must evaporate" and that "America will have to decide whose side it is on if only because the Arabs can now exert enough financial leverage and the Israelis sufficient military force, to make it choose."[60] The outcome on the occasion of the next Middle East war will be "to reverse the results of the previous one," with the U.S. "encouraging Israel to move into Libya and itself seizing Abu Dhabi and/or Kuwait [with] Saudi Arabia not an impossibility."[61] For those who shrink at such an exercise, resolve is to be instilled by viewing the alternative; i.e., "to let 200 years of Western civilization go by default."[62]

Though perhaps not of the highest priority among issues having to do with forcible intervention, the question of military feasibility must come first. To commit the kind of marine, army, and naval forces to the operation Ignotus' hapless informants designed would, during a period of obviously heightened tension throughout the world, create serious doubts about U.S. ability to meet its NATO and other security commitments. The activation of U.S. reserve forces and perhaps general mobilization would be required to fill the gap. This would create an attendant time span and glare of publicity hardly conducive to the kind of surprise postulated for seizing Gulf oil. As noted by a senior U.S. Army general who participated in actual study of U.S. military operations in the Gulf, the attack outlined by Ignotus bears some similarity to the pregnancy of an elephant—it takes a long time and is not easy to keep secret. A report by the Congressional Research Service of the Library of Congress, "Oil Fields as Military Objectives: A Feasibility Study," in August 1975 concluded that success would depend on two dubious prerequisites, "slight damage to key installations [and] Soviet abstinence from armed intervention," and that U.S. prospects would be poor, with plights of far-reaching political, economic, social, psychological, and perhaps military consequence the penalty for failure."[63] Pre-invasion sabotage, which Ignotus dismisses lightly, could have profound consequences for future production over an extended period with many unknowns looming in the event of fire in the uniquely high pressure Gulf wells. The Library's report estimates that two months from the day of alert would be required to "assemble, load, and move to the Middle East" a division-sized assault force from the Pacific."[64] Even if the assaults were unopposed, the British experience in Kuwait showed that personnel from temperate climates plunged into a desert environment suffer a high percentage of heat-induced casualties.

These newsworthy preparations plus similar activities in the U.S. to do with preparing reserve force human and physical assets would allow the target states ample time for careful preparation of their last minute destruction plans. They could also weigh diplomatic actions that in extremis could conceivably lead to the positioning of Soviet and/or other Eastern Bloc air defense units around key target areas. And as the Library's report succinctly concludes, "even if surprise were possible (a faint prospect in any crisis provoked by OPEC), U.S. parachute assault forces are too few to cover obligatory objectives quickly. Amphibious forces are too slow. Saboteurs could wreak havoc before they arrived."[65] A former head of ARAMCO with thirty-two years experience in Saudi Arabia estimates that Saudi sabotage of producing, transportation, and refining facilities would create damage requiring between one to three years for repair, irrespective of any possible harm to wells.[66]

Formidable as are the obstacles to seizure of the Arab fields in the Gulf, the problems of maintaining subsequent security on the ground, over the tanker sea-lanes, in the air corridors, and at refineries and pipelines in many areas of the globe would be even more overwhelming. In a world now coping only fitfully with a relative handful of terrorist groups, it is difficult to imagine that life in the Western nations could remain substantially unaltered were the Arab nations, with the rest of the Third World, turned into a recruiting base for terrorism and sabotage. Seventy-six percent of U.S. cruisers and destroyers would be required merely to convoy tankers from the Gulf through the Atlantic.[67] What would remain for other U.S. commitments, to say nothing of the tanker routes between the Gulf and Japan? In short, while intervention is technically feasible, it is difficult to imagine without bizarre political conditions within OPEC, a point where alternative courses of action would not be preferable to the West. The interventionists are wrong in their belief that the U.S. has not studied the implementation of punitive nonmilitary counteractions against OAPEC (Organization of Arab Petroleum Exporting Countries) and OPEC. Repugnant as they may be, they would represent Sunday school picnics by comparison to military seizure. Fortunately, as the interdependence between the well-being of the Gulf producing nations and the U.S. grows, the use by either side of punitive actions becomes less and less feasible.

The interventionists seem to share a philosophy of the desirable world order that is the real starting point of their solution. The Suez debacle of 1956 "was where America fought its friends—Britain, France and Israel—and supported its enemies—the Soviet Union and Egypt"; and "a good place to begin analyzing the decline of American foreign policy is the India-Pakistan war over Bangladesh, because all at once it revealed weaknesses that were to show up more slowly elsewhere."[68]

Apparently, then, the colonial era should never have concluded. The Suez canal should have remained occupied, and, presumably because the British were so foolhardy as to give up their Indian empire, U.S. forces should have been employed to support continued Pakistani mayhem in Bengal decades later. Despite, for instance, Tucker's admission that he is among those who "have argued for a radical contraction of America's interests and commitments," the use of armed force to solve economic and political problems emerges as his U.S. foreign policy matrix.[69] Instead of a world where U.S. influence leads toward greater accommodation among nations by negotiation and the expansion of commercial links, therefore, the interventionists would take us back to an imperial era in which the U.S. would act not so much as the world's policeman, but as its imperial czar, dispatching expeditionary forces to secure strategic natural resources or waterways whenever the natives misused their limited powers.

Apart from the great underlying misconception that every world evil, from unemployment in southern Italy to agricultural problems in India, could be put on the road to solution if only oil prices would drop, the interventionists' principal misreading of events rests in the perception of a precipitous loss of American power because of appeasement vis-à-vis OPEC. American power certainly has evolved in scope and independent capability due to the changing nature of the Atlantic alliance, the growth of Soviet conventional and nuclear power, and the advent of what has been an American goal since World War II—a greater degree of political and economic strength for the nations of the Third World. The interventionists, however, looking through the wrong end of their binoculars, see American power in the Middle East context as particularly weakened. One senses a longing for U.S. capability again to land marines on the beaches of Lebanon with impunity. Yet that time-buying military exercise occurred when the U.S. had but a fraction of its current ability to influence events in the Middle East. Thanks in part to Soviet errors, a U.S. presence is now practically as indispensable for Arab economic development and security posture as it is for Israeli. If the U.S. can maintain its role of relatively trusted broker in negotiations, it will continue to accrue far greater real power than it could by the exercise of a military option against the Gulf. Mistaken use of U.S. military power would herald the beginning of a golden Middle East era for the Soviet Union.

Fear of Arab leverage over the U.S. in the context of Arab-Israeli negotiations is a prime source of the interventionist motivation. Prospective Arab closings of the oil valves at the next crisis and a U.S. readiness to give in to Arab demands are equally assumed. The scenario presupposes that Israel has absolutely no concessions to make that do not fatally jeopardize her security, and therefore that any hint of Arab leverage on the U.S. is an anathema to Israeli security.[70] Prime Minister Begin's sudden shift in early 1978 from a security rationale to historical

justification for Israeli claims to portions of the occupied territories
exemplifies the emotionalism surrounding the issue. In fact, Israeli
security is most seriously jeopardized by immobility of the Middle East
problem, on one hand, and by any perceived capacity by either Arabs or
Israelis to dictate American Middle East policy, on the other.

No fact of American political life has been more amply demonstrated
during past years than the very substantial force of Israeli leverage
in the U.S. A recent professional analysis of U.S. public opinion polls
concluded that "a [U.S.] confrontation with Israel will create a deep
conflict within the United States, one that could very well parallel the Vietnam controversy in its bitterness, and that could have a devastating effect
on the popularity and the chances for reelection of those responsible."[71]

The far more recent growth of Arab leverage, based on a very
different but equally real circumstance, paradoxically represents a factor
working for resolution of the Arab-Israeli problem. Instead of harden-
ing since 1973, Arab negotiating positions have come to reflect in many
areas a new sense of compromise derived in part from enhanced
political poise and a new stake in stability. The positive manifestations of
moderate Arab leverage require recognition, therefore, in association
with efforts to keep oil prices down, to support moderate political forces
in the Middle East and the Horn of Africa, and toward peace settlement.
Arab leverage in this sense, within reasonable bounds, need be no more
a sinister force on American foreign policy than is Israeli leverage within
equally appropriate bounds. Only when one assumes that either the
Arabs or the Israelis intend to exercise economic or military force to
attain their goals in the same fashion contemplated for the U.S. by the
interventionists does the problem become unmanageable.

Above all, the U.S. cannot, as Friedland suggests, decide to be on
either the Arab or the Israeli side. The game is not cops and robbers.
The U.S. has vital interests on both sides, just as we have our differences
with both sides. Certainly, American policy differences with Israel
regarding the legality of settlements in occupied territories far predates
the recently acquired increase of Arab leverage. By expecting the
worst—utterly unreasonable Arab demands backed by embargo and
followed by an American incapacity to deal with the problem without
resort to force—the U.S. could conceivably bring about the worst by
allowing the return of polarization (Arab/Soviet and Israeli/U.S.) to the
Middle East.

U.S. security policy in the Gulf will continue to be affected by

Congressional concerns strongly influenced by the evolution of the Middle East negotiations. Of all these concerns, however, perhaps the least significant is the interventionists' assertion that U.S. military assistance and sales to the Gulf countries has been shortsighted in relation to a prospective U.S. invasion. Asked in 1974 why the U.S. was selling arms to the Saudis when American troops might become involved in combat there, Secretary of Defense Schlesinger replied, "In the extreme and highly unlikely circumstances which you have reiterated, it is not clear that American forces would prefer that they come face-to-face with equipment supplied by some other power as opposed to the United States."[72] In other words, familiarity with particular systems and the forces manning them would provide an advantage to an attacker that would be denied when confronting unfamiliar systems and forces. Schlesinger, of course, correctly presupposed that a U.S. refusal to provide military assistance and sales to Saudi Arabia would not result in a reduced level of Saudi force development.

QUESTION: *Sophisticated Weapons in the Gulf Increase the Risk of War and Are Militarily Pointless*

Underlying much of the criticism of U.S. Gulf security policy is the assumption, already noted, that war is more likely if adversary nations are well armed. The assumption is unsupported by evidence or even example, however, and is therefore elusive to pursue. Certainly, there is as much or more historical evidence to support the view that most wars have occurred because of an evident military weakness than because of an excess of strength. Recent conflicts in the Gulf area like the Yemeni civil war and the PDRY-supported insurgency in Oman occurred for strong historical reasons little influenced at their outset by quantities of weapons available on either side. The two best armed Gulf states, Iran and Iraq, came to the brink of war over circumstances that were more the cause of their arming than the result. As observed previously, the peaceful resolution of their conflicts in part reflected recognition by each that his adversary's strength precluded a military solution.

Some, however, like Senator Kennedy, believe that "the more heavily armed the various [Gulf] states become, the more likely it is that small disputes will be exacerbated by the presence and possible use of modern weapons."[73] Analysis of disputes in the area, past or present, tends, on the contrary, to support the view that small disputes are kept small when one or both sides become deterred by the possibility of significant retribution. Iraq's claim to parts of Kuwait surely is subdued by Iran's military capability, by growing Saudi force development, and by Kuwait's own activation of an air defense system with a fighter-bomber force, however modest. Iran's intervention in Oman, coupled with increasingly skillful and well-armed British-led Omani operations, helped prevent the small Dhofar insurgency from assuming far greater proportions as the costs for the PDRY became prohibitive.

The argument becomes at least superficially more compelling as mere quantity of weapons is refined to sophisticated weapons. With reference to the Gulf, one authority has written, "In fact, as the last two Arab-Israeli conflicts have demonstrated, the possession of highly sophisticated weapons by potential belligerents in explosive situations enhances the possibility that disagreements will be settled by fighting instead of diplomacy."[74] Are we to conclude that the prevalence of less sophisticated weapons in October 1973 might somehow have prevented the Arab attack on Israel? Such a hypothesis seems unsupportable. While the techniques of the attack and the Israeli response to it would have varied, the underlying Arab and Israeli political motivations presumably would have remained constant. Surprise, a highly sophisticated but scarcely modern weapon, formed the essence of Arab strategy. After the war, the Israelis not only revised their intelligence analysis procedures, but acquired more technologically sophisticated means to guard against repetition of a surprise attack. Rather than increasing the likelihood of another war, therefore, certain of these Israeli acquisitions serve as a further deterrent to Arab advocates of the military option.

The advent of the current generation of sophisticated U.S. weapons systems, which are in many cases an outgrowth of Vietnam, occurred in the same general time frame as the Gulf's transition away from British military protection. The two countries principally concerned with defense of the region, Iran and Saudi Arabia, both have viewed certain of the systems as particularly relevant to the military problems imposed by the combination of acute scarcity of skilled manpower and awesome geography. Saudi Arabia occupies a landspace nine times that of West Germany, a country approximately one-seventh the size of Iran. Without a coordinated mix of surface-to-air defense missiles, like the Hawk, and sophisticated interceptor aircraft, both countries would require older model aircraft and support personnel in prohibitively large numbers. The result, moreover, would be an inadequate air defense. Both Saudi Arabia's and Iran's basic sources of national wealth are concentrated in petroleum extraction and transportation facilities that create unique vulnerabilities to air attack. Yet, as already noted, both countries also have border threats that require the ability to respond over vast distances to points virtually around a full circle. Neither country, because of severity of terrain, can foreseeably develop the kind of extensive internal road and rail system typical of Western countries where there can be rapid surface movement of forces to all points. As a result, greatly increased mobility by air, and to the extent feasible, by ground, to permit small numbers of forces maximum effectiveness in a given area, has become a modernization priority.

Increased mobility and range of weapons systems provide each country with a greater ability to engage attacking forces long before they reach vital facilities. Targeting precision associated with new weapons systems reduces manpower demands as does the kind of multiplied capability exemplified by the F−14 (although the latter is one of Iran's more difficult programs), which with the Phoenix system can track 24 targets and fire on six of them simultaneously.[75] The Saudi decision to acquire 60 F−15 Eagle fighter aircraft and the subsequent controversy within Congress exemplifies clearly the mixture of technical misunderstanding and political motivations clouding the issue of arms sales to Gulf countries. The current Saudi air defense system, although improved during the past decade, contains significant gaps. Radar is obsolete, containing gaps for both low and high level detection. Saudi F−5Es, purchased as a transition aircraft, fulfill a close-in supporting role, but they do not qualify for all-weather or long-range night intercept. In contrast, the late model MiG−21s and MiG−23s flying in the inventories of Saudi Arabia's potential attackers have night and all-weather capability that would enable them, by flying at low altitudes, to approach key targets in the kingdom without detection.

By acquiring the F−15 to replace 46 British Lightning interceptor aircraft due for phase-out beginning in 1979, the Saudis plug many of these gaps with longer range intercept capability, wide radar coverage, all-weather missile launch capability, and significant protection against low altitude attacks by means of radar coverage at ground level combined with a follow-up missile capability.[76] Were the Saudis to have improved their air defense by opting for additional improved Hawk batteries alone, they would still not have achieved protection against low altitude attack and would have needed more than five times the number of personnel required for manning the 60 F-15s.[77]

Similarly, without the greater mobility and firepower being provided to the Saudi National Guard and army, the kingdom would have required increased numbers of forces prohibitive in relation to competing manpower requirements for economic development. Saudi naval development, which represents an initially heavy manpower drain due to its starting-from-scratch status, similarly stresses small, sophisticated, and specially designed vessels with sufficient range to move without refueling between the Persian Gulf and the Red Sea ports vital for Saudi trade and pilgrimage traffic—a distance of more than 2,500 miles. Without the sophisticated Harpoon surface-to-surface missile, these ships would have been virtually helpless in combat with the small missile-equipped ships of the Iraqi or PDRY navies.

Iran's modernization, based on a much broader spectrum of weapons systems in far greater numbers than the Saudi program, similarly stresses mobility and sophistication as offsets to space and manpower limitations. Iran's large investment in helicopters is designed to achieve a degree of mobility comparable to that available, for instance, in a country like France with an intensive road and rail network. P-3 Orion ocean surveillance and antisubmarine aircraft reduce the demand for a far larger number of surface combatants. Similarly, the controversial AWACS (Airborn Warning and Control System) aircraft could provide radar coverage that would otherwise require a vast network of costly ground radar installations.

Precision guided munitions (PGMs) form a central modernization emphasis for both Iran and Saudi Arabia, and are a major basis of definition for sophisticated weaponry. Despite numerous loose assertions regarding the impact of sophisticated weapons, particularly PGMs, on the military equation, current evidence suggests that the issue is very much open and that, as Cahn and Kruzel say, "No one knows whether [PGMs] will increase or reduce the risk of war in the 1980s and whether they will heighten or depress the level of damage if a war breaks out."[78] These analysts, in examining a series of propositions relevant to PGMs and arms trade, do, however, suggest that the current generation of PGMs creates a reliance by the buyer on the selling country that strengthens the military alliance under which they are associating. Of particular importance to the Persian Gulf is their observation that

"PGMs are far less complex and much easier to operate than many high-performance systems now being transferred," and that "on balance, PGMs appear to be a relatively stabilizing development in military technology [that] will be more appealing to states that feel threatened by tactical air and armor capabilities and somewhat less appealing to nations with offensive intentions."[79] Finally, these experts conclude that "systems that diminish the likelihood of surprise attack—including elaborate intelligence-gathering and surveillance systems using various types of sensors, electronic monitoring systems, and various types of reconnaissance aircraft—need to be identified; trade in such systems should be encouraged."[80] The pertinence of these systems to Gulf security and stability has already been noted. Iran's highly complex IBEX electronic intelligence gathering system and project SEEK SENTRY and PEACE SCEPTER communications and air defense radar integrating systems clearly fall in this category and yet have been generally classified by critics with lethal weapons and munitions.

Coupled with dogmatic and unsubstantiated assertions about the impact of sophisticated weapons in the Gulf, statements are frequently made that these weapons somehow pose additional risks because of poor command and control among the forces there.[81] The argument implies that some hotheaded unit commander will start a war by firing air defense missiles or ordering a jet fighter squadron to battle without national command authorization. While always possible, those Gulf states who are buyers of U.S. weapons appear among the least likely candidates in the world for such occurrences. Monarchies tend to be minutely exacting about the control of live ammunition and the movement of forces within their borders. Although air forces present special problems of control, anyone familiar with the workings of the Gulf military would attest to the extreme care and precision that are a hallmark. The weapons may be modern and sophisticated, but the techniques of control are ancient. Breaches of command and control appear, if anything, less likely than in the earlier days of scattered tribal forces dependent on far more primitive communications and weapons. The two Gulf states without monarchial governments, Iraq and the PDRY, personify tightly controlled, coup-prone environments in which the essence of government itself is defined by military control extending far down into the ranks.

Finally, the argument against modern weapons must ultimately rest on the existence of an alternative; i.e., non-modern weapons. On any reasonable scale and with any reasonably projected availability of spare parts and munitions, this option does not exist, even if the Gulf countries aspired to outdated military technology. Until political accommodation in the region and among the principal sellers of weapons reaches the stage where limitations can be agreed upon, modernization will continue. This does not mean, of course, that the industrialized countries need sell all their most sophisticated systems. Many are not required. The basic military modernization in the Gulf, however, is at present essentially without an alternative.

The costs are high, apart from money and manpower. In the understandable pursuit of greater independence, the buying country paradoxically becomes entangled in a very long-term dependent relationship with the selling country's technicians, training schools, spare parts, and munitions. The buyer runs the risk of permanent dependency if he insists on each new system that becomes available. Should he aspire to a self-sufficient indigenous technology and production base for weaponry, as has Iran, and the Arab states in principle, the investment will be astronomical over several generations, and the goal probably will remain illusory unless supported by a fully industrialized and scientifically self-sufficient economy.

QUESTION: *U.S. Military Support Contributes*
to Political Suppression

For many, the moral dimension becomes overridingly important when U.S. policy aims at increasing the military strength of states whose leadership is authoritarian. This issue requires far more forthright public discussion than it has thus far received. The impact of military programs is obviously quite different from that of economic development projects whose ultimate goal, irrespective of the nature of the recipient state's current political character, is to raise literacy and living standards. Economic programs readily imply creating an opportunity in which free political institutions may grow.

In contrast, military assistance programs merely postulate the sharing of a reasonably broad area of common values and purpose. In some cases, U.S. rationale rests more on direct self-interest where the alternatives to American military assistance are thought to jeopardize the security of the noncommunist community of nations. For the Gulf, it is clear that in the absence of a strong defense capability, the particular recipient country would become significantly more vulnerable to subjugation by truly totalitarian forces hostile to U.S. interests. While most Americans can readily identify significant areas of congruence between U.S. and Gulf national policies, the purposes of Gulf defense goals and America's stake therein remain obscured to wide public understanding.

Critics, in recognizing that Iran "is certainly by far the most powerful military force in the region," have then proceeded to say, "But the power of the state is brought about at the expense of the well-being of the Iranian people." In this sense they believe "American foreign policy is contributing to the suppression and the postponement of fundamental social changes in Iran."[82] The question is moot. The broadest practical issue for U.S. policy is whether we are to have close relationships throughout the world only with parliamentary democracies. If not, what degree of authoritarianism is acceptable in relation to the priority of our national self-interest? For a Uganda or a Rhodesia the analysis is simple. For the Gulf, where the U.S. has complex and vital security interests, the analyses are laden with dilemmas and hampered by profound limitations of knowledge.

Iran's economic achievements, spectacular as they are, combine with deficiencies almost as vivid. Saudi Arabia's starting point is well behind Iran's, its claims on its own behalf less strident, and its reins of power more shared. Iran therefore serves as a magnet for Western praise as well as criticism; from the standpoint of moral evaluation the measuring cup of Iran's accomplishments is either half full or half empty, depending on the viewer's predisposition. Does one focus on a GNP growth rate among the fastest in the world, stunning achievements in education at all levels, and infrastructural projects of unassailable significance for future generations? Or does one focus on highly limited freedom of political expression, on the urban clotting in Teheran, or the painfully slow trickle of economic benefits to many parts of the rural sector? U.S. foreign policy must reflect deep concern with such fundamental issues, irresolvable as they may be in the broader forum of U.S. public opinion. For the purposes of this study, however, we need merely weigh briefly the impact of overall U.S. policy on Iran and Saudi Arabia and then briefly assess the influence of U.S. military programs.

Conditions are imaginable in the Gulf where the U.S. might be forced to conclude that for a period of years Western security interests required a calculated support of truly retrogressive Gulf regimes in order to stabilize the flow of oil. Fortunately, there is little in Gulf politics to suggest such an assessment. Today, rather than fostering repression, the U.S. presence overall represents a potent catalyst for social and political change. Gulf aspirations for freer expression and political rights are nourished and stimulated by the thousands of Gulf students who have returned from the U.S., and by day-to-day contact with Americans working in the Gulf.[83] As a major contributor to economic development programs, the U.S. private sector stimulates the massive changes that are eroding tradition and forming new social groupings with obvious political implications. Although with good reason we should remain deeply skeptical about the value of American ambassadors giving lectures on government to monarchs, U.S. influence encourages the acceptance of democratic values at many levels, public and private. If a Gulf leader miscalculates and becomes the victim of a coup, radical or otherwise, surely analysts looking back will judge that U.S. policy on balance contributed more to the preceding conditions of ferment than it did to keeping the society static.

What of the particular impact of military modernization programs in which the U.S. plays such a prominent role? Surely we are beyond the stage where the kinds of sophisticated weapons systems being absorbed can be thought of as instruments of local repression. If a monarch is to crush a rebellion in one of his provinces, he does not require Hawk air defense missiles, Spruance class destroyers, or F−14 fighter-bomber aircraft. A case can be made, on the other hand, that increasing numbers of military create an ever more powerful segment of society which is financially and otherwise dependent on the monarch. Such a group presumably would resist a division of power in which the ruler's requests for defense expenditures would become subject to scrutiny by political factions interested in utilizing a greater proportion of resources on nonmilitary projects. Were the Gulf economies less dynamic and starved for skilled manpower this argument would merit more attention. The constant problem for the military leadership there, in fact, lies in retaining trained officers and lower grades.

Much of the existing analysis of Middle East armies for this reason does not fit the current Gulf situation. In downgrading the significance of armies as modernizing agents in the Middle East, for instance, J. C. Hurewitz finds that their career status, as opposed to conscript status, prevents significant feedback of skills into the civilian sector, that there are too few retirees to make a difference, and that the acquired skills of driving a truck or jeep are not applicable in villages.[84] Most Gulf countries are importing much of their labor force, including, as in Iran, manpower needed simply to drive trucks. But skills at all levels are sought on a highly competitive basis with the indigenous person naturally favored above the foreigner. The acquisition of English language skills, in addition to the kind of technical training associated with modern weapons systems, provides many military men in Iran or Saudi Arabia with access to the private sector at a salary often doubled. Under these conditions the potential national constituency for nonmilitary investment overshadows the military faction rather than the contrary situation that may occur in Middle East countries with stagnant economies.

In assessing the impact of Gulf military modernization, we should again remember history. Essentially, the military authority has been inseparable from the civilian, and there is today little grounds for assertion that the U.S. is injecting the Western virus of militarism into the Gulf. Authorities have long debated the particular impact of military modernization in the Middle East today. Some, like Halpern, have viewed the army as the "instrument of a new middle class committed to nationalism and social reform."[85] Others have taken a diametric view, asserting that such arguments emanate from U.S. official and corporate arms salesmen who wish to make their "product look attractive, to package . . . swords to look like plowshares."[86] Hurewitz maintains that, "in plural societies . . . officers by and large are not in fact social revolutionaries, even when they have seized political power," and concludes that we should ignore the claim that modern armies, "whether political or not, are modernizing agents at large in their societies."[87]

Regardless of whose analysis may be closer to the truth, social and economic conditions in the Gulf are sufficiently different to render the models based on countries like Egypt and Syria of little utility. While military modernization programs in the Gulf are indeed having a potent impact in the region, they are moving hand-in-hand with other equally if not more important changes in the civilian sectors of the economies. As to the political implications of an increasingly educated and skilled military in the Gulf, there is room for infinite speculation, but to date, scanty solid analysis. U.S. security policy can be as readily blamed for helping encourage forces of change as it can for not supporting the full spectrum of political rights. The risks for the U.S. are obvious, therefore, in utilizing the military assistance and sales instrument of foreign policy in the Gulf. The region is engaged in an unprecedented social and economic experiment for which there are no particularly useful past models. Given the overall impact of U.S. Gulf policy in its totality, however, there is little basis for American moral suffering on the supposition that our policy is the cause of a downturn in the welfare of the Gulf peoples, now or foreseeably.

QUESTION: *The World Energy Crisis is Fictional*

This view by Professor M. A. Adelman, whom *Foreign Policy* calls "a highly respected M.I.T. economist and oil expert," though expressed five years ago, continues to represent the thinking of a group of experts who cannot be ignored.[88] Adelman recently stated that "the crunch that Schlesinger talks about so eloquently is like the horizon—it recedes as you approach it."[89] Similarly, the International Trade Commission (ITC), an independent U.S. agency, contradicts the CIA analysis summarized earlier, and instead of serious energy shortages and price increases by 1985 predicts in a recent study that world oil supply and demand will remain in balance through 1985.[90] As noted by the *Wall Street Journal*, however, the ITC study indulges in a wholesale assumption that Saudi Arabia will as a political act continue to increase its production to meet world demand. Moreover, the ITC refuses to accept the CIA's evaluation of Soviet production trends, which CIA Director Stansfield Turner says is based on "highly sensitive intelligence sources unavailable to anybody else," thereby assuming that the Soviets will remain oil exporters through 1985.[91] Despite reports in *Business Week*, *Forbes*, and elsewhere in the media that the CIA has pulled back from its projections on Soviet production, the agency continues to support its original forecast.[92]

The potential impact of the variables involved is enormous considering that a Saudi decision to keep production at current capacities of 10 to 11 million barrels per day (bpd) would remove at least 8 to 9 million bpd from potentially available supplies by 1985. Should the CIA be correct rather than the ITC, the Soviets would move from a position of net exporters in the West of 1 million bpd today to that of net importers of between 3.5 and 4.5 million bpd by 1985. If the CIA is also correct that 1985 free world oil demand will be between 68.3 and 72.6 million bpd, the resulting 14.5 million bpd shortfall would represent 21 to 19 percent of total demand.

Resolution of divergent projections, however, if feasible at all, is not within the scope of this study. The variables involved are not only those derived from anticipating Saudi political intentions and Soviet extractive capability, but also Western and Japanese levels of industrial production, speed in developing alternate fuel sources, and success of energy conservation. From the contours of the problem we need to determine whether U.S. security is or is not vitally linked to the Persian Gulf regardless of which model is selected from the spectrum of responsible but differing judgments. First of all, Adelman's assertion that the energy crunch horizon recedes as it is approached holds perhaps temporary validity only in relation to world petroleum *reserves*. Reserves (except for those within the U.S.) are not the primary issue. The CIA's study casts no doubt on the acknowledged vastness of Soviet reserves. ARAMCO is reportedly discovering as much or more new oil in Saudi Arabia each year as is being produced from existing Saudi wells.[93] In the past, Adelman has both over- and underestimated the combined manipulative capabilities of OPEC and the oil companies. In the winter of 1972-73 he stated that "supply and demand have nothing to do with the world price of oil: only the strength of the cartel matters," and at the same time predicted that "an Arab boycott will hurt only the Arabs and soon collapse."[94] His view of the situation apparently still rests on a conspiratorial interpretation of State Department ignorance and bungling joining with company and cartel manipulations to create artificial scarcity in the midst of plenty. Careful study of production and consumption realities make this interpretation, however, appear not only simplistic, but somewhat irrelevant to the growing reality of U.S. dependence on imported oil.

Like Adelman, the ITC study disregards the variety of complex motivations of Saudi Arabia, the swing country in the production picture of the future, for increasing or not increasing the flow from its current 8.5 million bpd (with a capacity of about 11 million bpd) to the 19 to 23 million bpd the CIA believes the world will demand by 1985. Saudi policymakers, who are caught between the most stringent internal and external pressures, would no doubt sigh with relief if their one simple guideline were to maximize oil prices. In reality, of course, as informed news correspondents are beginning to report, Saudi policymakers are divided.[95] There are conservatives who prefer to limit production in order to slow the impact of social change on the kingdom, conserve for future generations, and avoid too large an investment commitment to foreign economies. On the other hand, the modernists, who generally prevail today, encourage rapid modernization at home by generating substantial oil revenues.

These modernists also view Saudi welfare as linked to the fate of moderate political forces in Egypt, Sudan, Syria, Jordan, the Horn of Africa, and much of the remaining Muslim world. The near infinite financial demands generated by these interests at some point conflict with equally compelling demands to restrain oil prices (by threatening to increase or actually increasing production) for the economic and political health of the Western democracies. As David Long indicates, this constraint, in turn, conflicts with the urgencies of the poorer OPEC members who require maximum revenues in a short time frame. Iran, for instance, with relatively meager reserves that may be exhausted by the year 2000, would predictably seek maximum prices coupled with the lowest feasible production.[96] Kuwait, on the other hand, although long interested in conserving its petroleum resources, depends on the natural gas output accompanying its oil production for domestic use. For Kuwait, therefore, too severe a cut in oil production would impact adversely on national economic prospects.[97]

Apart from the conflicting pulls of these various internal and external forces, the Saudis, viewing the entire problem from the perspective of unprecedented vast reserves, confront a parochial incentive to keep prices sufficiently low to ensure that development of alternate fuels is not so rapid as to leave Saudi Arabia with much of its potential wealth lying depreciated beneath the sands.[98] The complexity and force of these often divergent influences on Saudi production policy create an obvious need to be extremely wary of studies like the ITC's that postulate results out of hand. Equal wariness must be applied to those analyses based on a conspiracy approach in which the major oil companies and OPEC concert wantonly. Lack of unanimity between the major companies and the independents has been cited as an important factor leading to Libyan success in the fateful negotiations of 1970.[99] The majors today are subject, if anything, to even greater counterbalancing actions by the independents, to far greater scrutiny from Congress and federal authorities, and to the constant glare of national and international publicity. Paradoxically, constraints have increased for producers, companies, and consumers alike since the quantum price jump of 1973.

There are few general areas of consensus among energy analysts, but when pressed, most experts acknowledge that predictions beyond a five year time frame are necessarily subject to wide variation. Second, by 1985 U.S. oil imports, now at 8.79 million bpd, will range somewhere between the 9.6 million bpd estimated by the Petroleum Industry Research Foundation, Inc., the 11.8 million bpd by a June 1977 Library of Congress analysis, the 11.9 to 12.9 million bpd by a November 1977 General Accounting Office update (from a July prediction of 10.3 million bpd), and the 12.5 million bpd by Exxon.[100] Any of these amounts would represent a critical chunk of the estimated 22 to 25 million bpd oil demand projected for the U.S. by 1985.[101] Simply to meet Western demand in 1985, OPEC oil production will have to increase from its current 31 to 32 million bpd to 46 to 51 million bpd. The productive capacities of OPEC countries other than Saudi Arabia are not expected to increase except marginally, once again identifying the Saudis as pivotal.[102]

Even those on the low end of the projected import scale, like John Lichtblau, Executive Director of the Petroleum Industry Research Foundation, Inc., acknowledge the dominant position of Saudi Arabia, which he says could cut production and "create a shortage any time."[103] Harry B. Ellis, of the *Christian Science Monitor*, in fact, has found unanimity among experts dealing with the energy controversy to the effect that Saudi Arabia "hold[s] the key to the world's oil future."[104] The significance of Gulf resources for U.S. and European security, therefore, remains a constant among the welter of all but the most extreme judgments on energy forecasts.

As to the extreme positions that would deny the existence of a problem for U.S. security, we need to ask how such a large international body of expertise can be hoodwinked when the stakes are so huge. Ulf Lantzke, the Executive Director of the International Energy Agency, which is comprised of the principal consuming nations, stated at a recent conference, "All evidence shows that we are still confronted by a serious risk of an energy crisis in the 1980s. Beyond 1985, prospects are even bleaker."[105] Can we assume that the oil companies are so powerful as to have captured the principal energy ministers of the Western world? Similarly, widely diverging interpretation of Soviet production trends is to be expected because the extensive CIA studies are based in part on highly classified data. To dismiss entirely the possible impact of a Soviet production downturn, however, ultimately requires a judgment that the CIA and the many U.S. agencies contributing to its energy studies have been ordered by the administration to skew energy projections radically for the sake of easing the passage of energy legislation. Since the Soviets themselves acknowledge a problem, such a judgment taxes the imagination, even in this post-Vietnam, post-Watergate era.

Since the CIA studies, the Soviets announced that their 1978 oil production would barely exceed the 1977 level, a blow to the current five-year plan.[106] Reports circulate that the Soviets have informed some of the Eastern Bloc nations not to expect increases in oil supplies above the 1980 level.[107] The CIA's prediction in mid-1977 that the giant Soviet Samotlor field, which accounts for one-third of western Siberia's production, would soon peak caused worldwide comment. U.S. correspondents visiting Siberia early in 1978 were informed by the city Communist Party chief of Nizhnevartovsk, an administrative center for Samotlor, that "Samotlor would indeed peak next year . . . hold for seven or eight years . . . then drop, possibly sharply."[108] Samotlor in the past has accounted for most of Siberia's annual production growth.

A Soviet energy crunch, further, in adding to Soviet foreign exchange problems, would generate even greater pressures for arms sales. The CIA has noted that "as the economic function of arms sales becomes more vital to Soviet interests the Soviets are likely to become proportionally avid in seeking customers possessing hard currency or its oil equivalent."[109] Current Soviet willingness to sell arms even to impoverished countries, then, becomes the starting point from which it is reasonable to expect greatly increased sales efforts. The effects of such efforts on regional military balances throughout the world are alarming to imagine, particularly if combined with a self-imposed decline of offsetting U.S. military assistance activities.

Conclusion

British departure from the Gulf occurred almost as an afterthought to the major dismantling of empire. So late in coming, the act was greatly feared, not only in the West, but by many in the Gulf itself. For the most part, however, apprehensions have been replaced by a gradual growth of confidence. The specter of a power vacuum receded as the military competence of most of the Gulf countries progressed with major commitments of equipment and training from the West. Of even greater significance has been the gathering trend of cooperation—in resolving ancient disputes, in security matters, and in communications and environmental requirements. Doubtless, the spoiling role chosen by the Soviets—through the PDRY in Dhofar and through the subversive activities of Iraq and the PDRY throughout the Gulf—has quickened the pace of this cooperation.

Harder tests undoubtedly are yet to be faced in the Gulf. The initial surge of the post-1973 oil price boom has subsided and Iran's disturbances remind the Gulf of the social and political pressures that inevitably accumulate with transformation of the urban sector of an economy. Through technology and management services the U.S. remains in the forefront of foreign participation in these transformations. Without illusion, then, U.S. policy places first priority on economic development and secondarily supports Gulf security through several military instruments of foreign policy.

As both a cause and an effect of the growing equilibrium in the Gulf, defense modernization programs constitute a U.S. activity that cannot be replaced. The intrinsic military capability being imparted is only one aspect of the U.S. contribution. The symbolism of the U.S. defense-related presence conveys at least a capability if not always a readiness to offer logistics support to the Gulf in time of crisis. No other external power except the Soviet Union could substitute. Reduced opportunity for maintaining and establishing U.S. military bases in the Gulf area or its approaches creates obvious dilemmas for our defense posture. Military planners confront the acutely neuralgic concept of potential military contingencies in an arena of nightmarish inaccessability. U.S. capabilities, nonetheless, are equal to the challenge, assuming the requisite public support for adequately flexible military forces.

A wider equilibrium is being achieved. And the reciprocity of which every equilibrium is composed consists, for the West, in dependence on Gulf oil resources and a concurrent opportunity to sell large quantities of goods and services to help offset the financial consequences of this dependency. The Gulf countries, in turn, have become increasingly dependent on the financial health and stability of the West. Further, their interdependence on each other increasingly motivates decisions in the Gulf. Asymmetries of power have receded. The magnitude of Iranian population and military strength has been balanced by a growing Saudi Arabian financial and diplomatic capability of pivotal importance within and without OPEC. The strong continuity of Saudi religious conservativism, while making concessions to modernization, nonetheless helps sustain the kingdom's unique role in regional affairs and throughout the Islamic world. The smaller Gulf states have in one sense contributed to increased Saudi power and, in another, have as a group assumed a balancing role between Iran and Saudi Arabia. In the longer range, Gulf interests should continue to coalesce. The Saudi stake in Iranian development and stability is such that the much discussed advent of Iran's oil depletion now implies Saudi investment in Iran rather than the once-feared prospect of an Iranian seizure of Saudi wells.[1] Gulf political systems and rulers may change. Whoever leads, however, will face the same imperatives of interdependence. Even Iraq, hostage to Soviet military assistance, is nonetheless today constrained by certain of these imperatives.

The significance of U.S. policy achievements during this first phase of Gulf independence has but a tenuous hold on American public understanding. This tenuousness was displayed dramatically during the debates on the 1978 aircraft package sale to Egypt, Saudi Arabia, and Israel. For a policy that requires absolute consistency, the consequent risks are obvious. First, misunderstanding of the Gulf's role in world energy creates an unnecessary impediment to formation of a U.S. energy policy.

The unpleasant fact of dependency on the Gulf has been submerged under the broader category of foreign oil. Naturally, the full motivation behind U.S. actions in the Gulf are therefore not fully understood.

Second, broader U.S. interests are jeopardized. A weakened U.S. relationship with major Gulf states would injure the informally operative alliance that resists Soviet actions in the Horn of Africa and along the Red Sea. Israeli security would suffer through a strengthening of radical Arab forces in the Middle East in a manner sharply damaging to any peace settlement prospects.

The impediments to public understanding of the issues at stake arise from confusions about energy, about Israeli security needs, and about the practical effects of U.S.-assisted defense modernization in the Gulf. These are inevitable by-products of the American political system. Adding to these confusions is an even more profound and serious impediment. U.S. foreign policy doctrine has lost the ability to articulate convincingly that the U.S. has security interests abroad in non-NATO countries. This void perversely coincides with the particular U.S. and NATO dependence strikingly exemplified by the Gulf. The obscuring qualities of this void have been exacerbated by U.S. attacks on its own foreign policy actions in the military assistance area. The public is naturally confused.

President Carter's 1978 State of the Union message on the one hand cited our "first and prime [foreign policy] concern . . . the security of our country . . . based on our national will and on the strength of our armed forces," and on the other asserted without qualification that "our stand for peace is suspect if we are also the principal arms merchants of the world."[2] Allowance is not made for the urgent defense requirements of countries whose security impinges on U.S. well-being. For this reason, every arms sale or military assistance program is subject to the criticism of its creator even before its natural opponents can disapprove. Yet the military assistance instrument of foreign policy continues to be exercised in a variety of essential ways in Africa, the Middle East, and elsewhere.

This process displays a double standard that places top priority on U.S. military strength while denigrating as immoral the efforts of friendly nations to build their own strength. U.S. expressions of paternalism and self-righteousness cloud the urgent purposes of policy. The consequences are corrosive for the still-groping effort to redefine America's world role.

As Iran's crisis deepens—at a point nearly one year after basic completion of this study—the role of military assistance in U.S. policy moves into an even brighter limelight of controversy. Some observers cite perceived excesses in the Shah's defense modernization programs as a principal cause of his downfall. Others view a far more complex and intricate series of causative factors in which military programs were more symbolic than substantive. Regardless of perspective, there is no escape from the continuing need for the moderates in the Gulf area to develop adequate military strength. Iran's crisis has merely sharpened the edges of the debate. The problem for U.S. policy remains, if anything, at a new level of urgency.

Principal Characteristics of Major Weapons Systems

Aircraft | UNITED STATES

A—4M SKYHAWK II. The A-4 design concept grew from Korean War experience and was developed as a relatively simple, low-cost lightweight attack and ground support aircraft for the U.S. Navy and Marine corps. A more sophisticated version, the A—4M, was first delivered to the Marines in late 1970 as a single-seat attack bomber. Armament includes two 20 mm MK 12 cannons, each with 200 rounds of ammunition, and a wide variety of externally mounted bombs, air-to-air and air-to-surface missiles and rockets, ground attack gun pods, torpedoes, and countermeasures equipment up to about 7,700 lbs. Maximum level speed with a 4,000 lb. bomb load is 646 miles and maximum ferry range is 2,000 miles. Thirty-six have been sold to Kuwait.

F—4E PHANTOM. The F—4 was designed originally as a twin-engined, two-seat, long-range, all-weather attack fighter for the U.S. Navy, which took first delivery of the aircraft in December 1960. Many versions were developed. The F—4E evolved in response to U.S. Air Force requirements for a multirole fighter for air superiority, close support, and interdiction missions. The first F—4E production aircraft were delivered to the U.S. Air Force in October 1967, and subsequently, to the air forces of Israel, Greece, Turkey, Korea, and Iran. Most of these aircraft have since been retrofitted with wing leading-edge slats for improved maneuverability, and many F—4Es since 1973 have been fitted with target identification system electro-optical (TISEO), essentially a vidicon television camera with a zoom lens for positive identification of airborne or ground targets at long range. Typical F—4 armament would include Sparrow and Sidewinder air-to-air missiles, bombs, air-to-surface missiles or rockets up to

SOURCE: *Jane's All the World's Aircraft,* 1974—1975, 1975—1976, and 1976—1977 (London: S. Low, 1909—).

about 16,000 lbs. Maximum speed with armament load is more than Mach 2. Combat radius in interceptor role is more than 900 miles, and in ground attack role, more than 1,000 miles. Ferry range is 2,300 miles.

F−14 TOMCAT.   This multirole fighter is the most complex and sophisticated in the U.S. inventory. Its three primary missions are to (1) clear airspace for fleet attack forces, (2) defend carrier task forces with air patrol and interceptor operations, and (3) attack tactical targets on the ground supported by electronic countermeasures and fighter escort. The F−14 was first deployed with U.S. naval units in October 1972. Armament includes a 20 mm M61−A1 six-barrel Vulcan gun and the Phoenix missile system for use against air-to-surface and surface-to-surface missiles in a simultaneous four-missile launch against four targets. Various combinations of missiles and bombs up to 14,500 lbs. can be carried externally. The variable geometry wing facilitates takeoffs in less than 1,000 feet and maneuvers at below 86.5 mph. Maximum design speed is Mach 2.34. Service ceiling is above 56,000 feet. Iran has ordered 80 F−14s.

F−15 EAGLE.   The F−15 was designed specifically as an air superiority aircraft, but it has proved equally suitable for air-to-ground missions. The use of Fast Pack low drag attachable fuel pallets practically eliminates the need for tanker support during global deployment and permits carriage of heavier bomb loads to distant targets. Armament includes a 20 mm M61−A1 six-barrel Vulcan gun and a variety of air-to-air and air-to-surface missiles or rockets, and electronic countermeasures equipment up to 15,000 lbs. Deliveries of production aircraft to the U.S. Air Force began in November 1974. Absolute ceiling for the F−15 is 100,000 feet. Ferry range without Fast Packs is 2,878 miles, and with Fast Packs, 3,450 miles. Maximum speed is more than Mach 2.5.

F−16.   The F−16 was selected for full-scale engineering development in January 1975 for the U.S. Air Force's lightweight fighter program, whose specifications emphasized weight savings to meet critical performance categories of high acceleration rates and rate of climb, and exceptional maneuverability, which dictated limitations of aircraft size and use of advanced concepts to obtain optimum lift. The F−16's maximum external load of 15,200 lbs. typically configured could include six Sidewinder air-to-air missiles, two droptanks, a 2,200 lb. bomb, a laser tracker pod, single or cluster bombs, and air-to-surface missiles. Armament includes one 20 mm M61-A1 six-barrel Vulcan gun. Maximum speed at 40,000 feet is more than Mach 2.1. Service ceiling is above 50,000 feet. Radius of action is more than 575 miles. Ferry range with drop tanks is more than 2,303 miles.

F−5E.   The F−5E was selected as successor to the F−5A in November 1970 as an international fighter with emphasis on maneuverability rather than high speed. Deliveries to the U.S. Air Force for training purposes began in the spring of 1973, and to foreign countries in late 1973. The F−5E (Saudi) has a special internal navigation system and inflight refueling capability. Armament includes two M39A2 20 mm cannon and up to 7,000 lbs. of externally mounted mixed ordnance such as air-to-air missiles, rockets, and bombs. Maximum level speed is Mach 1.63. Service ceiling is 52,000 feet. Range with maximum fuel is 1,974 miles and without external tanks, 2,314 miles. Combat radius with two Sidewinder missiles and maximum fuel is 875 miles, or, with 6,300 lbs. of ordnance substituted for fuel, 190 miles.

P−3 ORION. Many new versions have followed the P−3's development as an anti-submarine warfare (ASW) aircraft in the late 1950s. The P−3C, the standard current version, carries a complex system built around a digital computer that integrates all ASW information and permits retrieval, display, and transmittal of tactical data to eliminate routine log-keeping functions. Newer P−3Cs carry improved avionics and software, including the OMEGA navigation system and two ARR-52A sonobuoy signal receivers. The P−3C normally is manned by a crew of ten. Maximum total weapon load includes six 2,000 lb. mines affixed under wings plus an internal load of 7,252 lbs. Weapons carried can include, in addition to mines, depth bombs and torpedoes. Sonobuoys and sound signals are launched from within the cabin. Maximum mission radius at 135,000 lbs. is 2,383 miles.

C−130H HERCULES. The C−130H version updated earlier Hercules models, with deliveries to the U.S. Air Force beginning in April 1975. The C−130H has been ordered by twenty-four foreign countries and is essentially a medium/long-range combat transport aircraft powered by four turboprop engines. Manned by a crew of four, with galley and sleeping quarters for a relief crew, the C−130H carries up to 64 paratroops or 92 regular troops. Larger weapons can be carried, such as the 155 mm howitzer with its high-speed tractor. Loading is expedited by the hydraulically operated main loading door and ramp at the rear cabin. Maximum cruising speed is 386 mph and maximum normal takeoff weight is 155,000 lbs. Range with maximum payload is 2,487 miles and with maximum fuel, 5,135.

Aircraft | GREAT BRITAIN

LIGHTNING F.MK53. The Lightning is a supersonic, all-weather, day-and-night interceptor produced originally for the Royal Air Force, with deliveries ending in 1967. The F.MK53 was built as an improved multirole ground attack fighter and operational trainer, with 34 sold to Saudi Arabia and 12 to Kuwait. First deliveries to Saudi Arabia were in December 1967. Armament includes two

30 mm Aden guns, and external ordnance can include 144 rockets or six 1,000 lb. bombs. Speed is more than Mach 2.

Aircraft | FRANCE

F1 MIRAGE.   The F1 is primarily an all-weather interceptor at any altitude. By January 1975, 280 had been ordered for the French and foreign air forces, with the first French unit becoming operational in early 1974. This single-seat multi-mission fighter and attack aircraft has two 30 mm DEFA 553 cannon and normally carries one air-to-air missile at each wingtip plus a variety of other external ordnance up to 8,820 lbs. For a ground-attack role a typical load would consist of one Martel anti-radar missile or AS.30 air-to-surface missile, eight 456 kg bombs, and four launchers, each containing 18 air-to-ground rockets or six 132 Imperial-gallon fuel tanks. Maximum high altitude speed is Mach 2.2, and low altitude speed is Mach 1.2. Endurance is 3 hours and 45 minutes.

Aircraft | USSR

MiG−15.   The MiG−15 was the first modern Soviet jet fighter, and began to appear in squadron service in 1949.

MiG−17.   The MiG−17 was a progressive development of the MiG−15 and was deployed in numbers during 1953 and 1954, to be followed by the MiG−19 in 1955.

MiG−21.   The MiG−21 design was based on combat experience between U.S. fighter aircraft and the MiG−15 during the Korean War. First versions were day fighters with limited range and comparatively light armament and limited avionics. Emphasis was on good handling, high rate of climb, with small size and light weight. Subsequent versions had improved range, weapons capability, and all-weather capability. These were sold to Iraq, Egypt, and Syria with search and track radar. Armament included one twin-barrel 23 mm gun with 200 rounds of ammunition. A typical load for an interceptor role would include two K−13 Atoll air-to-air missiles, two radar-homing advanced Atolls or two rocket packs (each with sixteen 57 mm rockets), and four advanced Atolls. A typical ground attack load would include four rocket packs, two 500 kg and two 250 kg bombs, or four 250 mm air-to-air Surf missiles. Maximum high altitude speed is Mach 2.1 and low altitude speed, Mach 1.06. Range with internal fuel is 683 miles. Ferry range with three external tanks is 1,118 miles.

MiG—23. The MiG—23 became operational in Soviet Air Force units in early 1972 and was sold to Egypt, Iraq, and Syria. The variable-geometry wing, tactical single-seat fighter is equipped with radar and missile systems comparable to the U.S. F—4 Phantom II. Armament includes one 23 mm twin barrel gun, and external ordnance can be added up to 8,000 lbs. Maximum speed at high altitude is Mach 2.3. Service ceiling is 59,000 feet and combat radius is 600 miles.

TU—95. The TU—95, which was first identified in July 1955, is a strategic attack bomber roughly comparable in role to the U.S. B—52. The TU—95 is in major service with the Soviet naval air force for maritime reconnaissance and to provide targeting data to the launch control and guidance stations responsible for both air-to-surface and surface-to-surface anti-shipping missiles. Six versions have been identified by NATO. Typical maximum takeoff weight would be 340,000 lbs. Maximum range with a 25,000 lb. bomb load is 7,800 miles.

Ships | UNITED STATES

TANG CLASS SUBMARINE. Six Tang class attack submarines were constructed between 1947 and 1949, of which two were transferred to Italy in 1973—4 and three are scheduled to be transferred to Iran. The original diesel engines were replaced in the late 1950s and the vessels modernized further in the 1960s with improved electronics equipment plus additional hull sections to bring overall length to 287 feet. The Tang normally carries eight 21-in. torpedoes, and has a speed of 15.5 knots surfaced and 16 knots dived. It has a crew of eleven officers and 75 enlisted men.

SPRUANCE CLASS DESTROYER. The Spruance destroyer is one of the newest and most complex U.S. naval vessels, whose primary purpose is anti-submarine warfare including operations as an integral part of attack carrier task forces. The Spruance is the first large U.S. warship to utilize gas turbine propulsion. The first ship was launched in November 1973. The Spruance's length is 529 feet, with a beam of 55 feet and 29 foot draught. Speed is more than 30 knots and range at 20 knots is 6,000 miles. Normal manning for the Spruance is 24 officers and 272 enlisted men. Armament includes two 5 in. 54 calibre (MK 45) single-barrel guns, and anti-submarine weapons include one SH-3 Sea King or two SH-2D Lamps helicopters, one ASROC 8 tube launcher, and two triple torpedo tubes (MK 32). Planned for installation are the NATO Sea Sparrow multiple missile launcher, two 20 mm Phalanx rapid-fire close-in

SOURCE: *Jane's Fighting Ships,* 1976—1977 (London: S. Low, 1898—).

weapons systems, and the Chaffrox (MK 36) system. Highly sophisticated
digital underwater fire control systems are utilized, coupled with similarly
advanced gunfire and missile control systems.

Missiles | UNITED STATES

HARPOON.   The Harpoon, for general surface ship fitting, carries a high
explosive warhead propelled by a solid fuel booster and a turbojet sustainer.
Weight is 1,110 lbs., length 15 feet, and range is 60 nautical miles. Guidance is
by preprogrammed active radar homing. The Harpoon is one of the newest
U.S. missiles.

SOURCE: *Jane's All the World's Aircraft,* 1971–1972, 1972–1973, 1975–1976 (London:
S. Low, 1909–).

Notes

Introduction and Chapter One

1. Sir Arnold T. Wilson, *The Persian Gulf: An Historical Sketch from the Earliest Times to the Beginning of the Twentieth Century* (Oxford: Clarenden Press, 1928), pp. 11–12.

2. Ibid., p. 1.

3. Philip K. Hitti, *History of the Arabs* (London: Macmillan & Co., 1949), p. 32.

4. Ibid., p. 59.

5. George Fadlo Hourani, *Arab Seafaring in the Indian Ocean in Ancient and Medieval Times* (Princeton, N.J.: Princeton University Press, 1951), p. 61.

6. Ibid., p. 83.

7. Donald Hawley, *The Trucial States* (London: Allen and Unwin, 1970), p. 53.

8. Ibid., p. 68.

9. Ibid., p. 72.

10. Robert Geran Landen, *Oman Since 1856: Disruptive Modernization in a Traditional Arab Society* (Princeton, N.J.: Princeton University Press, 1967), p. 10.

11. John R. Countryman, *Iran in the View of the Persian Gulf Emirates* (Carlisle Barracks, Penn.: U.S. Army War College, Military Studies Program Paper, May 7, 1976), p. 3.

12. Hawley, *The Trucial States*, p. 46.

13. Countryman, *Iran*, p. 13.

14. Wilson, *The Persian Gulf*, p. 112.

15. Ibid., p. 115.

16. Sir Rupert Hay, *The Persian Gulf States* (Washington, D.C.: Middle East Institute, 1959), p. 11.

17. Hawley, *The Trucial States*, p. 72.

18. H. Moyse-Bartlett, *The Pirates of Trucial Oman* (London: Macdonald, 1966), p. 20.

19. Hawley, *The Trucial States*, p. 94.

20. Ibid., p. 90.

21. Ibid., p. 102.

22. Ibid., pp. 96−98.

23. Ibid., p. 99.

24. John Marlowe, *The Persian Gulf in the 20th Century* (New York: Praeger, 1962), p. 20.

25. Wilson, *The Persian Gulf*, p. 269.

Chapter Two

1. R. J. Gavin, *Aden Under British Rule 1839−1967* (London: C. Hurst & Co., 1975), pp. 279−80.

2. Ibid.

3. Norman C. Walpole et al., *Area Handbook for Saudi Arabia* (Washington, D.C.: The American University, 1971), p. 323.

4. James Cable, *Gunboat Diplomacy: Political Application of Limited Naval Force* (London: Chatto and Windus, for the Institute of Strategic Studies, 1971), p. 47.

5. For a review of the controversies, see Ralph Hewins, *A Golden Dream: The Miracle of Kuwait* (London: W. H. Allen, 1963), pp. 288−305.

6. George Lenczowski, "Iraq: Seven Years of Revolution," *Current History*, Vol. 68, May 1975, pp. 281−89.

7. Gavin, *Aden*, p. 344.

8. Walpole, *Saudi Arabia*, p. 167.

9. Ibid., p. 166.

10. Hay, *The Persian Gulf*, p. 153.

11. John Morgan, "From Aden to Bahrain," *New Statesman*, February 25, 1966, p. 248.

12. David Holden, "The Persian Gulf: After the British Raj," *Foreign Affairs*, Vol. 49 (July, 1971), p. 722.

13. *Washington Star*, Vol. 49, January 17, 1968.

14. The Center for Strategic and International Studies, Georgetown University, *The Gulf: Implications of British Withdrawal* (Washington, D.C., Special Report, Series no. 8, February 1969), p. 3. The synopsis, which is the source of the quotation, was not cleared by the full group of specialists responsible for the Report.

15. Ibid.

16. Ibid.

17. *Manchester Guardian*, May 25, 1968; also see the Shah's reference to Gulf "weak governments, weak countries, subversion" (October 1969 NBC-TV "Meet

the Press," vol. 12, no. 41, Oct. 26, 1969) and his urging of the need to "replace rulers, reform medieval systems" (*Times* [London], April 13, 1970).

18. Holden, "The Persian Gulf," p. 724.

19. Ibid., p. 729.

Chapter Three

1. Rouhollah K. Ramazani, *The Persian Gulf: Iran's Role* (Charlottesville, Va.: University Press of Virginia, 1972), p. 50.

2. *Times* (London), June 30, 1969.

3. Ramazani, *Iran's Role*, p. 13.

4. Ibid., p. 411.

5. *Kayhan* (English daily, Teheran), January 6, 1969.

6. See J. B. Kelly's, *Eastern Arabian Frontiers* (London: Faber and Faber, 1964), p. 17, where, he points out, as of 1964, "the only internationally agreed territorial frontiers existent in Eastern Arabia today are those of Saudi Arabia with Kuwait and Iraq, laid down in 1922—23 when Britain was the mandatory power in Iraq, and, of more recent origin, the Saudi/Qatar frontier and some sectors of the boundaries of the Trucial Sheikhdoms with the Sultanate of Muscat and Oman. None of these frontiers has yet been formally demarcated on the ground."

7. Ibid., p. 19.

8. John Duke Anthony, "The Union of Arab Emirates," *Middle East Journal*, vol. 26 (Summer 1972), p. 280.

9. For a description of the Shatt al Arab issue see Shahram Chubin and Sepehr Zabih, *The Foreign Relations of Iran: A Developing State in a Zone of Great Power Conflict* (Berkeley: University of California Press, 1974), pp. 172—76.

10. R. M. Burrell and Alvin J. Cottrell, *Iran, the Arabian Peninsula and the Indian Ocean* (New York: National Strategy Information Center, 1972), p. 29.

11. Ibid.

12. Wilson, *The Persian Gulf*, p. 239.

13. D. L. Price, "Oman, Insurgency and Development," *Journal of Conflict Studies* (London: Institute for the Study of Conflict), p. 9.

14. In deference to Arab sensitivities over the use of Iranian forces in Oman, the Iranians were reportedly withdrawn in early October 1974 for several months to allow for the Rabat Summit of October 26—29, 1974.

Chapter Four

1. Georgetown University, *Implications of British Withdrawal*, p. 3.

2. James A. Bill and Carl Leiden, *The Middle East: Politics and Power* (Boston: Allyn & Bacon, 1974), p. 23.

3. See Hazem Zaki Nuseibeh, *The Ideas of Arab Nationalism* (Ithaca, N.Y.: Cornell University Press, 1956), for a cogent elaboration of this point on p. 112.

4. Bill, *Politics and Power*, p. 23.

5. *Times* (London), January 10, 1968.

Chapter Five

1. See Ramazani, *Iran's Role*, for a discussion of alternative Gulf security systems, p. 91.

2. *Times* (London), January 10, 1968.

3. Quoted from Shahram Chubin and Sepehr Zabih, *The Foreign Relations of Iran: A Developing State in a Zone of Great Power Conflict* (Berkeley: University of California Press, 1974), p. 237.

4. *Times* (London), March 4, 1968.

5. *Times* (London), June 10, 1969.

6. Chubin and Zabih, *Foreign Relations of Iran*, p. 191.

7. See interviews with the Shah in *Business Week*, November 17, 1975; *Kayhan International*, November 13, 1975; and *Le Monde*, March 1, 1976.

8. *New York Times*, May 1 and 2, 1978.

9. Chubin and Zabih, *Foreign Relations of Iran*, p. 193.

10. Cable, *Gunboat Diplomacy*, p. 229.

11. Chubin and Zabih, *Foreign Relations of Iran*, p. 191.

12. Subcommittee on Foreign Assistance, Committee on Foreign Relations, U.S. Senate, *U.S. Military Sales to Iran* (A Staff Report, July 1976, U.S. Government Printing Office, Washington, D.C.), p. 12.

13. Rouhollah K. Ramazani, *Iran's Foreign Policy 1941−1973: A Study of Foreign Policy in Modernizing Nations* (Charlottesville, Va.: University Press of Virginia, 1975), p. 405.

14. *Wall Street Journal*, August 24, 1977.

15. Ramazani, *Iran's Foreign Policy*, p. 104.

16. Sir Arnold T. Wilson, *Persia* (London: Ernest Benn, Ltd., 1932), pp. 152−53.

17. Ibid.

18. George Curzon, *Persia and the Persian Question* (London: Longmans, Green & Co., 1892, vol. 1), p. 587.

19. Ibid., p. 589.

20. Wilson, *Persia*, pp. 342−46.

21. George Antonius, *The Arab Awakening: The Story of the Arab National Movement* (Beirut: Khayat's College Book Cooperative, 1938), p. 346.

22. Ibid., p. 128. Denial of "modern" European weapons occurred as early

as 1914 when Abdullah (son of the Sharif of Mecca) asked Lord Kitchener for machine guns for use against the Turks.

23. Walpole, *Saudi Arabia*, p. 328.

24. The Information Section, Embassy of Israel, Washington, D.C., confirmed on January 23, 1978 continued Israeli occupation of the islands.

25. Walpole, *Saudi Arabia*, p. 321.

26. David E. Long, *The Persian Gulf: An Introduction to Its Peoples, Politics, and Economics* (Boulder, Colo.: Westview Press, 1976), p. 160.

27. Ibid.

28. *Washington Post*, June 22, 1973.

29. Stanford Research Institute, *Area Handbook for the Peripheral States of the Arabian Peninsula* (Washington, D.C.: The American University, 1971), p. 124.

30. Hawley, *The Trucial States*, p. 23.

31. Stanford Research Institute, *Area Handbook*, p. 152.

32. Landen, *Oman Since 1856*, p. 402.

33. Ibid.

34. *Washington Post*, September 17 and October 17, 1974.

Chapter Six

1. Joseph J. Malone, "America and the Arabian Peninsula: The First Two Hundred Years," *Middle East Journal*, vol. 30 (Summer 1976), p. 420.

2. James Forrestal, "Memorandum for the Secretary of State, Subject: Saudi Arabia" (RG 80, General Records of the Department of the Navy; Forrestal Files, Folder 36-1-30, August 1, 1945). For a detailed treatment of American petroleum policy in the Middle East during this period, see the forthcoming study by Irvine H. Anderson on *The Arabian American Oil Company and Middle Eastern Policy, 1933—1950*, intended for publication by Princeton University Press in 1979.

3. Walter Millis, ed., *The Forrestal Diaries* (New York: Viking Press, 1951), p. 323.

4. George Lenczowski, "United States' Support for Iran's Independence," *Annals*, vol. 401 (May 1972), p. 46.

5. George Lenczowski, *Russia and the West in Iran: A Study in Big-Power Rivalry* (Ithaca, N.Y.: Cornell University Press, 1949), p. 273.

6. Ramazani, *Iran's Foreign Policy*, pp. 158—60.

7. John A. De Novo, "American Relations with the Middle East During World War II: Another Watershed?" (University of Wisconsin, Madison, unpublished paper, July 1971).

8. Dillon Anderson to Eisenhower, July 24, 1957; Eisenhower to Anderson, July 30, 1957—Dwight D. Eisenhower Library, Abilene, Kansas. Quoted from

Burton I. Kaufman, "Mideast Multinational Oil, U.S. Foreign Policy, and Antitrust: the 1950's," *Journal of American History*, vol. 63, March 1977.

9. Ibid.

10. Department of State, Bureau of Public Affairs, *Gist*, May 1977. See also the *Wall Street Journal*, October 31, 1977.

11. Ibid.

12. *Wall Street Journal*, October 31, 1977.

13. Chevron, *Newsfront*, Winter 1978.

14. Ibid.

15. *Wall Street Journal*, April 20, 1978.

16. Central Intelligence Agency, *The International Energy Situation: Outlook to 1985* (ER 77-10240 U, April 1977), p. 1.

17. Ibid., pp. 1–2.

18. Ibid., pp. 12–13.

19. Ibid., p. 18.

20. Abraham S. Becker, *Oil and the Persian Gulf in Soviet Policy in the 1970's* (Santa Monica: The Rand Corporation, December 1971), p. 4.

21. Ibid., p. 17.

22. Standard Oil Company of California, July 1977.

23. See "Persian Gulf, Eastern Part 62390 and Persian Gulf, Eastern Part, Strait of Hormuz 62392," Defense Mapping Agency, Hydrographic Center, Washington, D.C., 20390. See also Congressional Research Service, Library of Congress, *Oil Fields as Military Objectives: A Feasibility Study* (Prepared for the Special Subcommittee on Investigations of the Committee on International Relations, Washington, D.C., August 21, 1975), p. 46; also John Cooley's May 2, 1978 article in the *Christian Science Monitor* on a proposed oil "interpol" in which he misconstrues the feasibility of blocking the strait with a sunken tanker.

24. Committee on Armed Services, U.S. Senate, *Soviet Military Capability in Berbera, Somalia* (Report of Senator Dewey Bartlett to the Committee on Armed Services, July 15, 1975).

25. *New York Times*, April 28, 1975.

Chapter Seven

1. Joseph J. Sisco, Statement before the Subcommittee on the Near East, House Committee on Foreign Affairs, August 8, 1972 (Department of State Bulletin no. 1732, September 4, 1972, vol. LXVII), p. 242.

2. Ibid., p. 243.

3. Robert R. Sullivan, "The Architecture of Western Security in the Persian Gulf," *Orbis*, vol. 14 (Spring 1970), pp. 79, 88–89.

4. Ibid., p. 81.

5. Anthony Harrigan, "Security Interests in the Persian Gulf and Western Indian Ocean," *Strategic Review* (Fall 1973), p. 13.

6. Committee on Armed Services, U.S. Senate, *Soviet Military Capability*; the Senator's team of experts who made an on-the-spot inspection of facilities at Berbera concluded that "The Department of Defense was remarkably accurate in their assessment of Soviet facilities . . . [being expanded] into a major military-capable, air and naval port," p. 1.

7. *Christian Science Monitor*, October 27, 1977.

8. James H. Noyes, testimony at Hearings before the Subcommittee on the Near East of the Committee on Foreign Affairs, House of Representatives, February 2, 1972, "U.S. Interests in and Policy Toward the Persian Gulf," p. 2.

9. Ibid., p. 13.

10. *Facts On File*, July 9, 1977, p. 2.

Chapter Eight

1. Leslie H. Gelb, "Arms Sales," *Foreign Policy*, XXV (Winter 1976—77), pp. 3—4.

2. H. C. Engelbrecht and F. C. Hanighen, *Merchants of Death: A Study of the International Arms Industry* (New York: Dodd, Mead & Co., 1934).

3. Comptroller, Defense Security Assistance Agency, *Worldwide Military Assistance Programs Breakout By Category and Year*, September 8, 1976.

4. Comptroller, Defense Security Assistance Agency, November 29, 1977.

5. Lee Hamilton, *U.S. Policy Toward the Persian Gulf*, The Congressional Record, June 21, 1973.

6. Robert E. Hunter, testimony, *New Perspectives on the Persian Gulf* (Hearings before the Subcommittee on the Near East and South Asia of the Committee on Foreign Affairs, House of Representatives, July 23, 1973), p. 106.

7. Edward Kennedy, "Persian Gulf: Arms Race or Arms Control," *Foreign Affairs*, vol. 54, Oct. 1975, p. 14.

8. Comptroller General of the U.S., *Foreign Military Sales: A Growing Concern* (Report to Congress, Washington, D.C., June 1, 1976), p. 14.

9. Marvin Zonis, 1973 Hearings, p. 105; see page 189 for Professor Zonis' biographic statement evidencing his extensive publications on Iran.

10. Joseph J. Sisco, testimony, *The Persian Gulf, 1975: The Continuing Debate on Arms Sales* (Hearings before the Special Subcommittee on Investigations of the Committee on International Relations, House of Representatives, June 10, 1975), p. 33.

1. U.S. Department of State, Iran and Arabian Peninsula Country Directorates, Washington, D.C., January 23, 1978.

12. E. A. Bayne and Richard O. Collin, *Arms and Advisors: Views from Saudi Arabia and Iran* (Hanover, N.H.: American Universities Field Staff, Southwest Asia Series, vol. 19, no. 1, July 1976), p. 5.

13. Sisco, 1973 Hearings, p. 33.

14. U.S. Department of State, Country Directorates.

15. Bayne, *Arms and Advisors*, p. 12.

16. *ARAMCO World Magazine*, January-February 1977, p. 14.

17. *Uniterra*, UN Environment Programme Newsletter, vol. 2, no. 1, December 1976-January 1977.

18. Ibid.

19. Hamilton, 1975 Hearings, p. *v.*

20. Hamilton, 1973 Hearings, p. 193, with reference to "The one concrete example of regional cooperation to which I can point is Iranian, Saudi Arabian, Jordanian, and Abu Dhabian participation in that nasty little rebellion in Oman."

21. Hunter, 1973 Hearings, p. 73.

22. Samuel P. Huntington, "Arms Races: Prerequisites and Results" (Cambridge, Harvard University, *Public Policy*, A Yearbook of the Graduate School of Public Administration, 1958), p. 51.

23. See Dale R. Tahtinen (with the assistance of John Lenczowski), *Arms in the Indian Ocean: Interests and Challenges* (Washington, D.C.: American Enterprise Institute for Public Policy Research, 1977), Appendix pp. 45–84 for tables of weapons inventories.

24. *Christian Science Monitor,* May 2, 1978.

25. American Universities Field Staff, *The Changing Balance of Power in the Persian Gulf,* Report of an International Seminar at the Center for Mediterranean Studies, Rome, June 26–July 1, 1972, p. 20.

26. Ibid., p. 25.

27. Samuel P. Huntington, *Political Order in Changing Societies* (New Haven: Yale University Press, 1968), p. 177.

28. Ibid., p. 199.

29. See Emile A. Nakhleh, *Bahrain: Political Development in a Modernizing Society* (Lexington, Mass.: Lexington Books, 1976), particularly pp. 76–85.

30. U.S. Embassy, Jidda, April 1977.

31. Muhammad T. Sadik and William P. Snavely, *Bahrain, Qatar and the United Arab Emirates: Colonial Past, Present Problems and Future Prospects* (Lexington, Mass.: Lexington Books, 1972), p. 28.

32. Ibid., pp. 121–22.

33. *New York Times*, April 25, 1975.

34. *Washington Post*, January 7, 1975 and *Christian Science Monitor*, January 10, 1975.

35. Comptroller General of the U.S., *Foreign Military Sales*, p. 14.

36. William B. Hankee, *The Role of Arms Trade in a Changing World Environment* (Carlisle Barracks, Penn.: U.S. Army War College, Strategic Studies Institute, December 1976), p. 14.

37. *New York Times*, March 3, 1977.

38. Following the infusion of $2.2 billion in U.S. military supplies committed to Israel after the October 1973 war, the U.S. intelligence community estimated that Israel would retain a widely sufficient edge decisively to defeat any combination of Arab enemies through 1980 without the addition of any further major weapons end items (as distinct from ammunition and other consumables). Additional billions in weapons orders for Israel have been authorized subsequently despite the projection of an increasing level of Israeli superiority beyond 1980.

39. Leonard A. Alne, 1975 Hearings, p. 191.

40. *New York Times*, October 20, 1977.

41. *New York Times*, October 1, 1977.

42. Emile A. Nakhleh, *The United States and Saudi Arabia: A Policy Analysis* (Washington, D.C.: American Enterprise Institute for Public Policy Analysis, October 1975), pp. 53–54.

43. *Analysis of the Saudi Arabian Request to Purchase F–15 Fighter Aircraft* (Department of Defense, unclassified summary, 1978), p. 7.

44. Ambassador James Akins, 1975 Hearings, p. 221.

45. Dale R. Tahtinen, *Arms in the Persian Gulf* (Washington, D.C.: American Enterprise Institute for Public Policy Research, 1974), p. 27.

46. Bayne, *Arms and Advisors*, pp. 13, 19.

47. Tahtinen, p. 27.

48. Robert Tucker, "Oil: The Issue of American Intervention," *Commentary*, January 1975, pp. 21–31 and "Oil and American Power: Three Years Later," *Commentary*, January 1977; Edward Friedland, Paul Seabury, and Aaron Wildavsky, *The Great Detente Disaster: Oil and the Decline of American Foreign Policy* (New York: Basic Books, Inc., 1974); Miles Ignotus, "Seizing Arab Oil," *Harpers Magazine*, March 1975, pp. 45–62.

49. Ignotus, ibid., p. 45.

50. Ignotus, ibid., pp. 52, 58.

51. Ignotus, ibid., p. 62.

52. Ignotus, ibid., p. 58.

53. Tucker (Jan. 1975), ibid., p. 21.

54. Ibid., p. 23.

55. Ibid., p. 25.

56. Tucker (Jan. 1977), ibid., p. 30.

57. Ibid., p. 35.

58. Friedland, ibid., p. 3.

59. Ibid., p. 75.

60. Ibid., pp. 20, 70.

61. Ibid., p. 20.

62. Ibid.

63. Congressional Research Service, *Oil Fields as Military Objectives*, p. 76.

64. Ibid., p. 59.

65. Ibid., p. 75.

66. *Los Angeles Times*, April 13, 1975, Thomas Barger.

67. Congressional Research Service, *Oil Fields as Military Objectives*, p. 66.

68. Friedland, *The Great Detente Disaster*, pp. 29, 58.

69. Tucker, *Oil: American Intervention* (Jan. 1975), p. 28.

70. For professional military analysis of Israel's boundaries in relation to security see Colonel Merrill A. McPeak, "Israeli Borders and Security," *Foreign Affairs*, Vol. 54 (April, 1976), pp. 426–43; General Mattityahu Peled, "Dissociating Israeli Security from More Territory," *New York Times*, December 16, 1977, p. A31.

71. Martin Seymour Lipset and William Schneider, "Carter vs. Israel: What Polls Reveal," *Commentary*, November 1977, p. 29; see also the *New York Times* November 6, 1977 editorial, "The Jews and Jimmy Carter."

72. Department of Defense, News Release, January 14, 1974, News Conference, The Pentagon.

73. Kennedy, "Persian Gulf," p. 25.

74. Tahtinen, *Arms in the Persian Gulf*, p. 30; see also an unpublished study by Paul C. Kinsinger, "The Black Watch: Arms and Security in the Persian Gulf," December 30, 1973, in which he concludes, "The area is potentially volatile because of the oil industry and will become increasingly more so as the various Gulf states arm themselves with more and more sophisticated weapons," p. 42.

75. *Aviation Week and Space Technology*, January 31, 1977.

76. Department of Defense, unclassified summary, 1978.

77. Ibid.

78. Ann Hessing Cahn et al., *Controlling Future Arms Trade* (New York: McGraw Hill; 1980's Project, Council on Foreign Relations, 1977), p. 52 in "Arms Trade in the 1980's" by Cahn and Kruzel.

79. Ibid., pp. 52–57.

80. Ibid., pp. 100–01.

81. Kennedy, "Persian Gulf," p. 24, and Hunter, 1973 Hearings, p. 73.

82. Zonis, 1973 Hearings, pp. 64–65.

83. The *International Herald Tribune*, Feburary 1978, reported 10,000 Saudi Arabian students studying in the U.S., and the Jackson Report (*Access to Oil—The United States Relationships with Saudi Arabia and Iran*, prepared at the request of Senator Henry M. Jackson, Chairman, Committee on Energy and Natural Resources, U.S. Senate, December 1977), on p. 88 refers to 25,000 Iranian students in the West.

84. J. C. Hurewitz, *Middle East Politics: The Military Dimension* (New York: Frederick A. Praeger, 1969), p. 430.

85. Manfred, Halpern, "Middle Eastern Armies and the New Middle Class," in *The Role of the Military in Underdeveloped Countries*, John J. Johnson, ed. (Princeton, N.J.: Princeton University Press, 1962), pp. 277–315.

86. Hurewitz, *Middle East Politics*, p. 434.

87. Hurewitz, ibid., pp. 428, 430.

88. M. A. Adelman, "Is the Oil Shortage Real?" *Foreign Policy* (Winter 1972-73, no. 9), p. 73.

89. M. A. Adelman, *New York Times*, January 18, 1978.

90. *Wall Street Journal*, September 13, 1977.

91. Ibid.

92. Confirmed by the CIA's Development and Analysis Center, Office of Economic Research, April 4, 1978. See *Business Week*, December 19, 1977 and *Forbes*, March 6, 1978. CIA's report, *The Soviet Economy in 1976–77 and Outlook for 1978*, released in October, 1978, maintains the position that "Soviet oil output will peak within the next few years and then begin a long decline," as reported in the *Christian Science Monitor*, October 4, 1978.

93. *Christian Science Monitor*, August 29, 1977.

94. Adelman, "Is the Oil Shortage Real?", pp. 90, 94.

95. *Christian Science Monitor*, February 2, 1978.

96. Long, *The Persian Gulf: An Introduction*, p. 96.

97. Long, ibid., p. 97.

98. Long, ibid., p. 97.

99. Richard Chadbourn Weisberg, *The Politics of Crude Oil Pricing in the Middle East 1970–1975: A Study in International Bargaining* (University of California, Berkeley, Institute of International Studies, Research Series no. 31, 1977), p. 51.

100. U.S. Bureau of Mines (for U.S. import figure), and the *New York Times*, November 3, 1977 (for U.S. import projections).

101. Central Intelligence Agency, *International Energy Situation*, p. 15.

102. Central Intelligence Agency, ibid., pp. 15–16.

103. *Christian Science Monitor*, February 7, 1978.

104. Ibid.

105. *Christian Science Monitor*, October 11, 1977.

106. *Wall Street Journal*, January 9, 1978.

107. Ibid.

108. *Christian Science Monitor*, January 23, 1978.

109. Central Intelligence Agency, *Soviet Economic Problems and Prospects* (July 1977, ER 77-10436 U), p. 28.

Conclusion

1. See Joseph J. Malone's lead article in "Focus on Saudi Arabia," Part Two, *International Herald Tribune*, February, 1978.

2. *New York Times*, January 20, 1978.

Bibliography

Abbas, Kelidar. *Iraq: The Search for Stability*. London: Institute for the Study of Conflict, Conflict Studies no. 59, 1975.

Abir, Mordechai. *Oil, Power and Politics: Conflict in Arabia, the Red Sea and the Gulf*. Portland, Oregon: International Scholarly Book Services for Frank Cass & Co., 1974.

Abu Jaber, Kamal. *The Arab Baath Socialist Party*. Syracuse, N.Y.: Syracuse University Press, 1966.

Albaharna, Husain M. *The Arabian Gulf States: Their Legal and Political Status and their International Problems*. Beirut: Librairie Du Liban, 1975.

American Universities Field Staff. *The Changing Balance of Power in the Persian Gulf*. Report of an international seminar at the Center for Mediterranean Studies, Rome, June 26–July 1, 1972.

Anthony, John Duke. *Arab States of the Lower Gulf: People, Politics, Petroleum*. Washington, D.C.: Middle East Institute, 1975.

———. "The Union of Arab Emirates." *Middle East Journal*, vol. 26, Summer 1972.

Antonius, George. *The Arab Awakening*. Beirut: Khayat's College Book Cooperative, 1938.

Badeau, John S. *The American Approach to the Arab World*. New York: Harper & Row, 1968.

Barger, Thomas C. *Arab States of the Persian Gulf*. Washington, D.C.: American Enterprise Institute, 1974.

———. *Energy Policies of the World—Arab States of the Persian Gulf*. Newark, Del.: University of Delaware, Center for the Study of Marine Policy, 1975.

Bausani, Allessandro. *The Persians*. New York: St. Martin's Press, 1962.

Bayne, E. A. and Collin, Richard O. *Arms and Advisors: Views from Saudi Arabia and Iran*. Hanover, N.H.: American Universities Field Staff, Southwest Asia Series, vol. 19, no. 1, 1976.

Beasley, R. "The Vacuum That Must Be Filled—The Gulf and Iran's Military Potential Assessed." *New Middle East*, no. 32, May 1971.

Berger, Morroe. *The Arab World Today*. New York: Doubleday, 1962.

———. *Military Elite and Social Change: Egypt Since Napoleon*. Princeton, N.J.: Center of International Studies, 1960.

Bill, James A. and Leiden, Carl. *The Middle East: Politics and Power*. Boston: Allyn and Bacon, 1974.

Bujra, Abdalla S. *The Politics of Stratification: A Study of Political Change in a South Arabian Town*. Oxford: Oxford University Press, 1971.

Burrell, R. M. "Iranian Foreign Policy: Strategic Location, Economic Ambition and Dynastic Determination." *Journal of International Affairs*, vol. 29, no. 2, 1975.

———. *The Persian Gulf*. Georgetown, Va.: Washington Center for Stragetic Studies, 1972.

Burrell, R. M. and Cottrell, Alvin J. *Iran, the Arabian Peninsula and the Indian Ocean*. New York: National Strategy Information Center, 1972.

Busch, Briton Cooper. *Britain and the Persian Gulf 1894—1914*. Berkeley: University of California Press, 1967.

Cable, James. *Gunboat Diplomacy: Political Application of Limited Naval Force*. London: Chatto and Windus, for the Institute for Strategic Studies, 1971.

Cahn, Ann Hessing. "Have Arms, Will Sell," *Arms Control Today*, vol. 4, no. 10, October 1974.

Cahn, Ann Hessing et al. *Controlling Future Arms Trade*. New York: 1980's Project/Council on Foreign Relations, McGraw Hill, 1977.

Carpenter, William M. and Gilbert, Stephen P. *Great Power Interests and Conflicting Objectives in the Mediterranean, Middle East and Persian Gulf Region*. Arlington, Va.: Strategic Studies Center, Stanford Research Institute, 1964.

Central Intelligence Agency. *The International Energy Situation: Outlook to 1985*. ER 77-10240 U, April 1977.

———. *Prospects for Soviet Oil Production*. ER 77-10270, April 1977.

———. *Prospects for Soviet Oil Production: A Supplemental Analysis*. ER 77-10425, July 1977.

Chubin, Shahram. "Iran's Security in the 1980's." *International Security*, Harvard University, vol. 2, no. 3, Winter 1978.

Chubin, Shahram and Zabih, Sepehr. *The Foreign Relations of Iran: A Developing State in a Zone of Great Power Conflict*. Berkeley: University of California Press, 1974.

Churba, Joseph. *Conflict and Tension Among the States of the Persian Gulf, Oman, and Saudi Arabia*. Maxwell Air Force Base, Ala.: Air University Documentary Research Study, AV-204-71-IPD, December 1971.

Cottam, Richard W. *Nationalism in Iran*. Pittsburgh: University of Pittsburgh Press, 1964.

Countryman, John R. *Iran In the View of the Persian Gulf Emirates.* Carlisle Barracks, Penn.: U.S. Army War College, Military Studies Program Paper, 1976.

Curzon, George. *Persia and the Persian Question.* London: Longmans, Green & Co., 1892.

Daniels, John. *Abu Dhabi: A Portrait.* London: Longman, 1974.

——. *Kuwait Journey.* Luton, Beds.: White Crescent Press, 1971.

Darby, Philip. "Beyond East of Suez." *International Affairs,* vol. 46, no. 4, October 1970.

Drambyantz, G. "The Persian Gulf: Twixt the Past and the Future." *International Affairs,* Moscow, no. 10, October 1970.

Eliezer, Beeri. *Army Officers in Arab Politics and Society.* New York: Praeger, 1970.

Engelbrecht, H. C. *One Hell of a Business.* New York: Robert M. McBride & Co., 1934.

Engelbrecht, H. C. and Hanighen, F. C. *Merchants of Death.* New York, Dodd Mead & Co., 1934.

Fenelon, K. G. *The United Arab Emirates: An Economic and Social Survey.* London: Longman, 1973.

Field, Michael. "The New Gulf Power." *Mid-East International,* no. 9, December 1971.

Fisher, Sydney N., ed. *The Military in the Middle East: Problems In Society and Government.* Columbus, Ohio: Ohio State University Press, 1963.

Friedland, Edward, Seabury, Paul, and Wildavsky, Aaron. *The Great Detente Disaster; Oil and the Decline of American Foreign Policy.* New York: Basic Books, 1975.

Furlong, R. D. "Iran: A Power To Be Reckoned With." *International Defense Review,* December 1973.

Gavin, R. J. *Aden Under British Rule 1839–1967.* London: C. Hurst & Co., 1975.

Gelb, Leslie H. "Arms Sales." *Foreign Policy,* no. 25, Winter 1976–77.

Georgetown University. *The Gulf: Implications of British Withdrawal.* Washington, D.C.: The Center for Strategic and International Studies, special report series no. 8, February 1969.

Gerasimov, O. "Foreign Bases On the Arabian Peninsula." *International Affairs,* Moscow, no. 12, December 1963.

Gibb, Sir Hamilton and Bowen, Harold. *Islamic Society and the West.* London: Oxford University Press, 1950.

Glubb, John B. *The Conflict of Traditionalism and Modernization in the Muslim Middle East.* Edited with introduction by Carl Leiden from papers delivered March 29–31, 1965. Austin, Texas: University of Texas, 1965.

The Gulf Committee. *Documents of the National Struggle in Oman and the Arabian Gulf.* London: 1974.

Haddad, George Meri. *Revolutions and Military Rule In the Middle East.* New York: Robert Speller, 3 vols., 1965–73.

Halliday, Frederick. *Arabia Without Sultans.* New York: Vintage Books, 1975.

Halpern, Manfred. "Middle East Armies and the New Middle Class" in *The Role of the Military in Underdeveloped Countries,* John J. Johnson, ed., Princeton, N.J.: Princeton University Press, 1962.

Hankee, William B. *The Role of Arms Trade In a Changing World Environment.* Carlisle Barracks, Penn.: U.S. Army War College, Strategic Studies Institute, 1976.

Harrigan, Anthony. "Security Interests in the Persian Gulf and Western Indian Ocean." *Strategic Review,* Fall 1973.

Havens, Murray C., Leiden, Carl, and Schmitt, Karl M. *The Politics of Assassination.* Englewood Cliffs, N.J.: Prentice Hall, 1970.

Hawley, Donald C. *The Trucial States.* London: Allen & Unwin, 1970.

Hay, Sir Rupert. "The Impact of the Oil Industry On the Persian Gulf Shaykhdoms." *Middle East Journal,* Autumn 1955.

———. *The Persian Gulf States.* Washington, D.C.: The Middle East Institute, 1959.

Hewins, Ralph. *A Golden Dream: The Miracle of Kuwait.* London: W. H. Allen, 1963.

Hitti, Philip K. *History of the Arabs.* 4th rev. ed. London: Macmillan, 1949.

Holden, David. "The Persian Gulf: After the British Raj." *Foreign Affairs,* vol. 49, July 1971.

Hopwood, Derek, ed. *The Arabian Peninsula: Society and Politics.* Totowa, N.J.: Rowman and Littlefield, 1972. See particularly "Problems and Prospects of Development in the Arabian Peninsula," by Yusif A. Sayigh, pp. 286–300.

Hourani, George Fadlo. *Arab Seafaring In the Indian Ocean In Ancient and Early Medieval Times.* Princeton, N.J.: Princeton University Press, 1951.

Hunter, Robert E. *The Soviet Dilemma in the Middle East, Part II: Oil and the Persian Gulf.* International Institute of Strategic Studies, Adelphi Papers no. 60, October 1969.

Huntington, Samuel P. "Arms Races: Prerequisites and Results," Harvard University *Public Policy,* Yearbook of the Graduate School of Public Administration, 1958.

Hurewitz, J. C. "The Persian Gulf: British Withdrawal and Western Security." *Annals,* vol. 401, May 1972.

———. *The Persian Gulf: Prospects for Stability.* Foreign Policy Association, Headline Series no. 220, 1974.

———. *Middle East Politics: The Military Dimension.* New York: Praeger, 1969.

Ignotus, Miles. "Seizing Arab Oil." *Harpers Magazine,* March 1975.

Jukes, Geoffrey. *The Indian Ocean in Soviet Naval Policy.* International Institute of Strategic Studies, Adelphi Papers, no. 87, May 1972.

Al-Karmi, Hasan. "The Prophet Muhammad and the Spirit of Compromise." *Islamic Quarterly*, vol. 8, December 1974.

Kelly, J. B. *Eastern Arabian Frontiers*. London, Faber and Faber, 1964.

Kennedy, Edward. "Persian Gulf: Arms Race or Arms Control." *Foreign Affairs*, vol. 54, October 1975.

Khadduri, Majid. *Political Trends in the Arab World: The Role of Ideas and Ideals in Politics*. Baltimore: Johns Hopkins Press, 1970.

———. "The Role of the Military in Middle East Politics." *American Political Science Review*, vol. 47, no. 2, June 1953.

King, Gillian. *Imperial Outpost—Aden: Its Place in British Strategic Policy*. London: Oxford University Press, Chatham House Essays under the Auspices of the Royal Institute of International Affairs, 1964.

Kinsinger, Paul. "Arms Purchases in the Persian Gulf: The Military Dimension." Printed in *The Persian Gulf, 1975: The Continuing Debate on Arms Sales*, Hearings Before the Special Subcommittee on Investigations of the Committee on International Relations, House of Representatives, 94th. Congress, June 10, 18, 24, and July 29, 1975, U.S. Government Printing Office: 1976, p. 229. Also useful is an unpublished study, "Arms and Security in the Persian Gulf," completed in Fall 1973.

Knauerhase, Ramon. *The Saudi Arabian Economy*. New York: Praeger, 1975.

Landen, Robert Geran. *Oman Since 1856: Disruptive Modernization in a Traditional Arab Society*. Princeton, N.J.: Princeton University Press, 1967.

Lenczowski, George. *Russia and the West in Iran, 1918—1948: A Study in Big Power Rivalry*. New York: Cornell University Press, 1949.

———. "The Oil Producing Countries." *Daedalus*. vol. 104, Fall 1975.

———. *Middle East Oil in a Revolutionary Age*. Washington, D.C.: American Enterprise Institute, 1976.

———. "Iraq: Seven Years of Revolution." *Current History*, May 1965.

———. "United States' Support for Iran's Independence." *Annals*, vol. 401, May 1972.

Lipset, Martin Seymour and Schneider, William. "Carter Vs. Israel: What the Polls Reveal." *Commentary*, vol. 64, no. 5, November 1977.

Liska, George. *Imperial America: The International Politics of Primacy*. Baltimore: Johns Hopkins Press, 1967.

Looney, Robert. *The Economic Development of Iran*. New York: Praeger, 1973.

Long, David E. "U.S. Gulf Policy." *Current History*, vol. 68, January 1975.

———. *The Persian Gulf: Introduction to its People, Politics, Economy*. Boulder, Colo.: Westview Press, 1977.

———. *Saudi Arabia*. Washington, D.C.: Georgetown University Center for Strategic and International Studies, The Washington Papers, 39, 1976.

Mabro, Robert and Monroe, Elizabeth. "Arab Wealth from Oil: Problems of its Investment." *International Affairs*, vol. 50, no. 1, January 1974.

Malone, Joseph J. "America and the Arabian Peninsula: The First Two Hundred Years." *Middle East Journal*, vol. 30, Summer 1976.

Marlowe, John. *The Persian Gulf in the Twentieth Century.* New York: Praeger, 1962.

The Middle East Institute. *The Arabian Peninsula, Iran and the Gulf States: New Wealth, New Power,* a conference on Middle East affairs. Washington, D.C.: 1973.

Mikdashi, Zuhair. *The Community of Oil Exporting Countries.* New York: Cornell University Press, 1972.

Miles, S. B. *The Countries and Tribes of the Persian Gulf.* Portland, Ore.: Frank Cass & Co., 1966.

Millis, Walter, ed. *The Forrestal Diaries.* New York: Viking press, 1951.

Monroe, Elizabeth. *Britain's Moment in the Middle East 1914–1956.* London: Chatto and Windus, 1963.

———. *The Changing Balance of Power in the Persian Gulf.* Report of an International Seminar at the Center for Mediterranean Studies, Rome, June 26–July 1, 1972; New York, American Universities Field Staff, 1972.

Moyse-Bartlett, H. *The Pirates of Trucial Oman.* London: Macdonald, 1966.

Nakhleh, Emile A. *Bahrain: Political Development in a Modernizing Society.* Lexington, Mass.: Lexington Books, 1976.

———. *The United States and Saudi Arabia: A Policy Analysis.* Washington, D.C.: American Enterprise Intitute, 1975.

Nordlinger, Eric A. "Soldiers in Mufti: The Impact of Military Rule Upon Economic and Social Change in the Non-Western States." *American Political Science Review,* vol. 104, no. 4, December 1970.

Nuseibeh, Hazem Zaki. *The Ideas of Arab Nationalism.* New York: Cornell University Press, 1956.

O'Neill, Major Bard E. USAF. *Petroleum and Security: The Limitations of Military Power in the Persian Gulf.* National Defense University, Research Directorate Monograph 77-4, October 1977.

Pranger, Robert J. and Tahtinen, Dale R. *Toward a Realistic Military Assistance Program.* Washington, D.C.: American Enterprise Institute, 1974.

Ramazani, Rouhollah K. *Iran's Foreign Policy 1941–1973: A Study of Foreign Policy in Modernizing Nations.* Charlottesville, Va.: University Press of Virginia, 1975.

———. *The Persian Gulf: Iran's Role.* Charlottesville, Va.: University Press of Virginia, 1972.

———. *The Foreign Policy of Iran: A Developing Nation in World Affairs 1500–1941.* Charlottesville, Va.: University Press of Virginia, 1966.

———. "Iran and the United States: An Experiment in Enduring Friendship."

Middle East Journal, vol. 76, Summer 1976.

————. "Iran's Search for Regional Cooperation." *Middle East Journal*, vol. 30, Spring 1976.

Rugh, William. "Emergence of a New Middle Class in Saudi Arabia." *Middle East Journal*, vol. 27, Winter 1973.

Sadik, Muhammad T. and Snavely, William P. *Bahrain, Qatar and the United Arab Emirates: Colonial Past, Present Problems and Future Prospects.* Lexington, Mass.: Lexington Books, 1972.

Sisco, Joseph J. Statement of U.S. Gulf Policy before the Subcommittee on the Near East of the House Committee on Foreign Affairs. Department of State Bulletin, vol. 68, no. 1732, September 4, 1972.

Smolansky, Oles M. "Moscow and the Persian Gulf: An Analysis of Soviet Ambitions and Potential." *Orbis*, vol. 14, Spring 1970.

Sullivan, Robert R. "The Architecture of Western Security in the Persian Gulf." *Orbis*, vol. 14, Spring 1970.

Thompson, George G. *Problems of Strategy in the Pacific and Indian Oceans.* New York: National Strategy Information Center, 1970.

Tucker, Robert. "Oil: The Issue of American Intervention." *Commentary*, January 1975.

————. "Oil and American Power: Three Years Later." *Commentary*, January 1977.

Uriel, Dann. *Iraq Under Qassem: A Political History 1958–1963.* New York: Praeger, 1969.

Vali, Ferenc A. *Politics of the Indian Ocean Region: Balances of Power.* New York: The Free Press, 1976.

Vatikotis, P. J. *The Egyptian Army in Politics: Pattern for New Nations.* Bloomington, Ind.: Indiana University Press, 1961.

Vicker, Ray. *Kingdom of Oil.* New York: Scribner, 1974.

Villiers, Alan. "Some Aspects of the Arab Dhow Trade." *Middle East Journal*, October 1948.

Wall, Patrick. "The Persian Gulf—Stay or Quit?" *Brasseys Annual: Defense and the Armed Forces, 1971*, Major General J. L. Moulton, ed. London: William Clowes, 1971.

Walpole, Norman C. et al. *Area Handbook for Saudi Arabia.* Washington, D.C.: The American University, 1971.

Weisberg, Richard Chadbourn. *The Politics of Crude Oil Pricing in the Middle East, 1970–1975: A Study in International Bargaining.* Berkeley: Institute of International Studies, University of California, Research Series, no. 31, 1977.

Wells, Donald A. *Saudi Arabian Development Strategy.* Washington, D.C.: American Enterprise Institute, 1976.

Wilson, Sir Arnold T. *Persia.* London, Ernest Benn Ltd., 1932.

————. *The Persian Gulf: An Historical Sketch from the Earliest Times To the Beginning of the Twentieth Century.* Oxford: Clarenden Press, 1928.

Winstone, H. V. F. and Freeth, Zahra. *Kuwait: Prospect and Reality.* London: Allen and Unwin, 1972.

Yar-Shater, Ehsan, ed. *Iran Faces the Seventies.* New York: Praeger, 1969.

Zonis, Marvin. *The Political Elite of Iran.* Princeton, N.J.: Princeton University Press, 1971.

Zartman, I. William, Paul, James A., and Entelis, John P. "An Economic Indicator of Socio-Political Unrest." *International Journal of Middle East Studies,* October 1971.

Index

A—4M fighter bomber aircraft, 41, 77
Abadan (Iran), 20, 32
Abha (Saudi Arabia), 66
Abu Dhabi, 22, 39, 40, 73
Abu Musa (Persian Gulf island), 18
Aden Colony, 10, 12, 14
Afghanistan, 7f, 32
Albuquerque, 4—5
American Persian Gulf Command, 45
Arab-Israeli dispute: relationship to Gulf, xvi; impact on Gulf of 1948 Palestine war, 9, 24; impact of 1967 war on Saudi Arabian strategy, 37; and oil equation, 46; potential to radicalize Gulf states, 74; military balance, 74—75
Arab League, 11
Arabi, al- Island (Persian Gulf), 17
Arabian American Oil Company (ARAMCO), 36, 107
Asir Province (Saudi Arabia), 13
AWACS, 100

Baghdad Pact, 43
Bahrain, 22, 26; ancient entrepôt, 2; Iran's claim to, 4, 17; Qatar invasion threat in 1859, 8; British troops transferred from Aden, 14; middle class, 24; riots in 1956, 25; headquarters for British Gulf Command, 25—26; size of military forces, 39; description of U.S. naval facility, MIDEASTFOR, 54, 56—58; political role of indigenous labor force, 71—72; duration of family rule, 73
Baluchistan, 34
Bandar Abas (Iran), 58
Begin, Menachem, 95

Boumedienne, Houari, 20
British in the Persian Gulf: rule assessed, xvi; policy influence of Aden experience, 13; policy, lack of unanimity on, 14—15; diplomacy in creating neutral zone between Saudi Arabia and Kuwait, 29; naval occupation of Kharg Island, 32; military presence in Oman after 1971, 41
Bubiyan Island (Kuwait), 10, 22
Buraimi Oases, 9, 19
Byrnes, James, 45

C—130 transport aircraft, 77
Canton, 2
Central Treaty Organization (CENTO), 23, 31, 58
China, Peoples Republic of, 21
Cuba, 21, 52, 68

Dhofar insurgency, Oman, 21, 41, 97, 123n13
Diego Garcia (Indian Ocean island), 56
Dubai, 22, 73

East Germany, 21, 68
Egypt, 12f, 51
Eisenhower, Dwight, 45
Eritrea, 51
Ethiopia, 52

F1 Mirage fighter bomber, 79
F—104 fighter aircraft, 36

F−4 Phantom fighter bomber, 83
F−5E fighter bomber, 38
F−14 Tomcat fighter bomber, 84, 99, 104
F−15 Eagle fighter bomber, 79, 85, 99
Faisal, King, 13, 19, 73
Farsi (Persian Gulf island), 17
Ford, Gerald, 33
France, 8, 79−80
Frog missile, 32

Harpoon missile, 100
Hawk missile, 36, 91, 98
Hejaz Province (Saudi Arabia), 35
Hormuz, city state, 3, 5
Hormuz, Strait of, 18, 41, 50
Horn of Africa, 51

India: military role with British, 5, 11−
    12; volunteers in Oman, 21; increase
    in military capability, 33; reported med-
    dling among Pakistan tribes, 34; Soviet
    pressure on for bases, 55; potential for
    arms race with Iran, 70; laborers in
    Saudi Arabia, 72
International Energy Agency, 109
International Trade Commission, 106f,
    109
Iran: origin of claim to Bahrain, 17; mil-
    itary role in Dhofar insurgency, 22;
    relations with Israel, 31; size of mil-
    itary forces, 38; beginnings of coop-
    eration with U.S., 45
Iran-Arab relations, 1, 16, 54, 89
Islam, 2−3
Ismail, Abdul Fattah, 37
Iraq: ancient trade center, Ur, 2; Saudi
    raids on, 9; claim to Kuwait, 10, 98;
    activism in Gulf, 14; proposal for Arab
    defense organization in Gulf, 30; intro-
    duction of weapons in Gulf, 32; re-
    action to U.S. basing, 55; reasons for
    military buildup, 69
Israel: potential for intervention in Gulf,
    27; cooperation with Iran supporting
    Kurds in Iraq, 30; special relations with
    Iran, 31; security in relation to U.S.
    arms sales to Gulf, 80−82; concessions
    and security, 95; political leverage in
    U.S., 96

Japan, 27, 49
Jordan, Hashemite Kingdom of: partici-
    pation in Arab League defense of Ku-
    wait, 11; joint defense council with
    Saudi Arabia, 1962, 14, 36; military role
    in Dhofar insurgency, 21−22; military
    assistance to Gulf, 40, 42; exemplifies
    successful U.S. military assistance, 77

Kassem, General Abd al Karim, 10f
Khalifa, al-, 73
Kharg Island, 8, 32
Khasmi, al-, General Ahmed, 37
Khorramshahr, 8, 20
Khuzistan Province, Iran, 20, 33
King Abd al Aziz University, 66
Kissinger, Henry, 91
Kurds, rebellion of: 20, 30, 33, 69
Kuwait: and British, 8, 12; and Iraq, 10;
    middle class, 24; size of military forces,
    39; welfare state in, 73

Lebanon, 73
Lightning fighter bombers, 36
Lingeh (Persian city), 5

Maldives, 56
Masirah Island (Oman), 58
Mecca, 66
MIDEASTFOR. See Bahrain
MiG 15 and 17, 32
MiG 21, 39
Mossadeq, Muhammad, 14
Musandam Peninsula (Oman), 50
Muscat, 5, 7f

Nadir Shah, 17
Nasser, Gamal Abdal, 13
North Atlantic Treaty Organization
    (NATO), xiii, 27, 49, 93
Neutral Zone, between Saudi Arabia and
    Kuwait, 29
Nixon, Richard, 33

Organization of Arab Petroleum Ex-
    porting Countries (OAPEC), 94
Ogaden Province (Ethiopia), 51
OKEAN 1975, 52
Oman, Sultanate of, 4f, 9, 40. See also
    Dhofar insurgency

Organization of Petroleum Exporting Countries (OPEC), 108; projected production increase, 47; Saudi Arabian price leverage on, 50; interventionist approach toward, 90–91; U.S. options against, 94; manipulative capabilities of, 107
Ottoman Empire, 9

P–3 Orion aircraft, 100
Pakistan: military role in Oman, 21; significance of East Pakistan severance for Gulf, 33; and Baluchi separatism, 34; new Iran relationship, 70; laborers in Saudi Arabia, 72
Palestine, 73
Palestinians, 24
Popular Front for the Liberation of Palestine (PFLP), 70
Popular Front for the Liberation of the Occupied Arab Gulf, 21
Persian Gulf: early significance, 1; Portuguese arrival in, 4; foreign military, use of, 5, 9, 34; treaties, 6, 8, 10, 13, 17; disputes among ruling families, 22; internal security in sheikhdoms, 26; military cooperation, 41; intelligence exchange, 70; early frontiers, 123n23
Petroleum Industry Research Foundation, 109
Philippine laborers, 72
Piracy, Persian Gulf, 3, 5, 7
Portugal, 3, 5
Precision Guided Munitions (PGMs), 100–101

Qais, 3
Qatar, 8, 17, 22, 39, 73
Qawasim, 5–6
Qishm (Persian Gulf island), 6

Ras al Khaimah, 5, 18. *See also* Qawasim
Red Sea, 2
Roberts, Goronwy, 30
Rome, 2f
Rubaye, Ali Salem, 37

Samotlor, 110
Saud, Abd al Aziz Ibn, 9, 35
Saudi Arabia, Kingdom of: military participation in Arab League, 11; objection to British in Aden Colony, 12; joint defense council with Jordan, 14; recognition of United Arab Emirates, 19; financial aid to Oman, 22; security threat from the Yemens, 37; size of military forces, 38; oil production, 47; leverage on OPEC, 50; national guard, 66; economic development, 66; foreign labor force, 72; military pilot capability, 89
Schlesinger, James, 91
Shah (Mohammad Reza Shah Pahlevi), 16, 18, 122, 123n17
Sharjah, 26. *See also* Qawasim
Shatt al Arab, 10, 20, 123n9
Sinafir Island (Strait of Tiran), 37
Siraf, 3
Socotra Island, 4
Somalia, 51
South Africa, 55
South Korean laborers, 72
Soviet Union, 68; introduces modern weapons, 11–12; in North Yemen civil war, 13; in Dhofar insurgency, 21; diminution of wider Middle East influence, 27; post–World War II pressure on Iran, 35; energy imports, 48; military activities, 51–52, 55–56
Spruance class destroyer, 62, 104
Styx missile, 32
Sultan, Prince Ibn Abd al Aziz, 77
Syria, 33, 69

Tabuk (Saudi Arabian city), 66
Taif Pact, 36
Tang Dynasty, 3
Taraki, Noor Mohammad, 32
Tiran Island, 37
Trade Routes, 2–3
Trucial Oman Scouts, 39–40
Tunb Islands, 18
Turkish laborers, 72

Um Qasr (Iraqi port), 10–11
United Arab Emirates (UAE), 19, 22f, 39–40
United Nations, 4, 18, 67–68
United States: begins Saudi Arabian air force training, 1947, 36; early cooperation with Iran, 45; oil imports and consumption, 46–47; intelligence facilities in Iran, 56; Military Assistance Advisory Groups, 61–62; Army Corps of

Engineers in Saudi Arabia, 63; civilian and military presence in Saudi Arabia and Iran, 65–66, 87; Department of Defense commitment for logistics support, 82; petroleum policy in Middle East, 1933–1950, 125n2
University of Riyadh, 66–67

Wadia, al- (Saudi Arabian town), 39
Wahabis, 8
Warbah (Persian Gulf island), 10, 22
Water resources: in Persian Gulf, 23

Yemen, North: early control of trade, 4; 1962 revolution, 12; Soviet role in 1966–67 civil war, 13; attacks on Saudi Arabia, 1962, 14; impact of civil war on Saudi Arabia, 36; as Nasser's path to Saudi Arabian oil, 36; Jordanian military personnel in, 42; laborers in Saudi Arabia, 72
Yemen, Peoples Democratic Republic of (PDRY), 39, 55, 71

Zayd, Shaykh bin Sultan Al Nuhayyan (President of United Arab Emirates), 19

DATE DUE			